COMPACT *Research*

Immigration

Current Issues

ReferencePoint
Press®

San Diego, CA

COMPACT *Research*

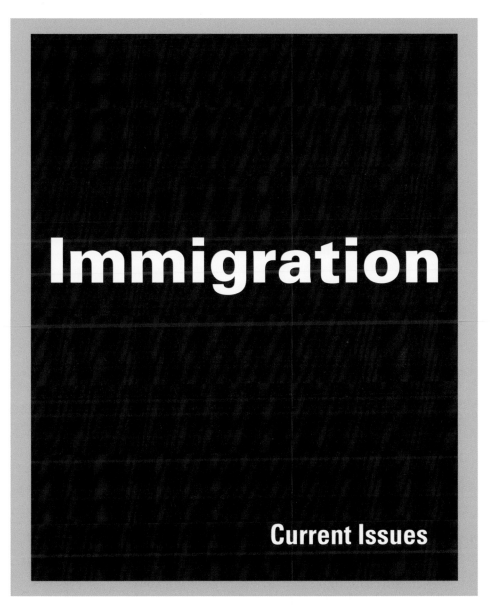

Immigration

Current Issues

ReferencePoint Press®

San Diego, CA

*For a complete list of titles please visit www.referencepointpress.com.

COMPACT *Research*

Immigration

by Andrea C. Nakaya

Current Issues

ReferencePoint
Press®

San Diego, CA

© 2010 ReferencePoint Press, Inc.

For more information, contact:
ReferencePoint Press, Inc.
PO Box 27779
San Diego, CA 92198
www. ReferencePointPress.com

Picture credits:
Cover: Dreamstime and iStockphoto.com
Maury Aaseng: 35–36, 49–52, 65–67, 79–82
AP Images: 14, 21

LIBRARY OF CONGRESS CATALOGING-IN-PUBLICATION DATA

Nakaya, Andrea C., 1976–
    Immigration / by Andrea C. Nakaya.
      p. cm. —(Compact research series)
    Includes bibliographical references and index.
    ISBN-13: 978-1-60152-095-1 (hardback)
    ISBN-10: 1-60152-095-6 (hardback)
    1. Emigration and immigration—Government policy. 2. Illegal aliens. I. Title.
    JV6035.N35 2009
    304.8'73—dc22

                                                                    2009023404

Contents

Foreword

> **"Where is the knowledge we have lost in information?"**

—T.S. Eliot, "The Rock."

As modern civilization continues to evolve, its ability to create, store, distribute, and access information expands exponentially. The explosion of information from all media continues to increase at a phenomenal rate. By 2020 some experts predict the worldwide information base will double every 73 days. While access to diverse sources of information and perspectives is paramount to any democratic society, information alone cannot help people gain knowledge and understanding. Information must be organized and presented clearly and succinctly in order to be understood. The challenge in the digital age becomes not the creation of information, but how best to sort, organize, enhance, and present information.

ReferencePoint Press developed the *Compact Research* series with this challenge of the information age in mind. More than any other subject area today, researching current issues can yield vast, diverse, and unqualified information that can be intimidating and overwhelming for even the most advanced and motivated researcher. The *Compact Research* series offers a compact, relevant, intelligent, and conveniently organized collection of information covering a variety of current topics ranging from illegal immigration and deforestation to diseases such as anorexia and meningitis.

The series focuses on three types of information: objective single-author narratives, opinion-based primary source quotations, and facts and statistics. The clearly written objective narratives provide context and reliable background information. Primary source quotes are carefully selected and cited, exposing the reader to differing points of view. And facts and statistics sections aid the reader in evaluating perspectives. Presenting these key types of information creates a richer, more balanced learning experience.

For better understanding and convenience, the series enhances information by organizing it into narrower topics and adding design features that make it easy for a reader to identify desired content. For example, in *Compact Research: Illegal Immigration*, a chapter covering the economic impact of illegal immigration has an objective narrative explaining the various ways the economy is impacted, a balanced section of numerous primary source quotes on the topic, followed by facts and full-color illustrations to encourage evaluation of contrasting perspectives.

The ancient Roman philosopher Lucius Annaeus Seneca wrote, "It is quality rather than quantity that matters." More than just a collection of content, the *Compact Research* series is simply committed to creating, finding, organizing, and presenting the most relevant and appropriate amount of information on a current topic in a user-friendly style that invites, intrigues, and fosters understanding.

Immigration at a Glance

Current Levels

Immigration is the primary source of population growth in the United States. An estimated 37 million legal immigrants are in the country—about 12 percent of the population.

Hispanic Immigrants

Hispanics are the dominant immigrant group, currently 14 percent of the population and expected to increase to 29 percent by 2050.

Immigration and the Economy

While some people insist that immigration contributes to economic growth, others argue that immigrants take American jobs, drive down wages, and overuse public benefits.

Link with Crime

Many people believe immigration—especially undocumented immigration—increases the level of crime in the United States, yet a number of studies show a correlation between immigrants and a reduction in crime.

National Security

Critics fear that potential terrorists are able to enter the United States too easily, yet others point out that because of the sheer number of immigrants entering the country every year, tightening security enough to eliminate this risk completely may be impossible.

Health Care and Education

How immigrants impact both education and health care is a controversial subject. Critics charge that they lower the quality and increase the cost of these services for U.S. citizens, but others insist that immigrants contribute more to society than they take from it.

Immigration Reform

While the majority of Americans call for immigration reform, such reform has been impossible due to a lack of public consensus on how it should take place.

Illegal Immigration

It is generally agreed that deporting the country's estimated 12 million undocumented immigrants would be impossible and undesirable, yet views on how to deal with the issue of illegal immigration differ widely.

Increased Enforcement

Federal border enforcement budgets have increased substantially in the past few years, and the level of state action regarding immigration is unprecedented; in 2008, 206 state immigration laws were enacted.

Overview

66History has shown that immigration encourages prosperity.99

—*The Economist*, weekly newspaper.

66Americans are paying a huge price for our government's . . . open door policies.99

— American Legion, veterans organization.

Immigration is a major public concern in the United States. The majority of people believe the current system needs to be reformed. For example, according to a June 2007 report by the Pew Research Center, only 7 percent of those surveyed believed immigration laws do not need changing. However, disagreement about the impacts of the current system and how it should be changed is widespread.

Historical Perspective

Throughout history, the United States has vacillated between welcoming and resenting immigrants. The country has integrated tens of millions of immigrants; however, numerous periods of anti-immigrant sentiment have also occurred. For example, in the mid-1800s the United States welcomed its first great wave of immigrants, many of whom were escaping social and political unrest in western and northern Europe, but the large numbers of Irish who entered the country faced widespread anti-Irish sentiment. In the late-nineteenth and early-twentieth centuries, another wave of immigrants came—more than 23 million—many from eastern and southern Europe. Natives then became concerned that these eastern and southern Europeans were becoming too large a percentage of the population, and the United States instituted the national-origins quota system, which effectively excluded future southern and eastern European immigrants.

Rates of immigration have fluctuated throughout history and are now at a record high. With some exceptions, the number of immigrants to the United States generally increased from the 1820s to 1910, when immigrants accounted for a record high of 14.7 percent of the population. Then, as a result of decades of low immigration, the foreign-born population dropped to a record low of 4.7 percent in 1970. Since then, immigration has increased again, and in 2008 was again at record levels, with an estimated 37 million immigrants living in the United States, or 12 percent of the population.

Who Can Immigrate?

In order to immigrate to the United States, a foreign citizen must file an immigrant petition. A petition must be based on one of a number of categories of eligibility; for example, a foreign citizen might be eligible to immigrate if he or she has a relative who is a U.S. citizen or legal permanent resident, or has found a U.S. employer willing to provide a job. Once an application is approved, the prospective immigrant may live and work anywhere in the United States, own property, and attend public schools, colleges, and universities. He or she may later apply to become a U.S. citizen if certain eligibility requirements can be met.

> **The majority of people believe the current [immigration] system needs to be reformed.**

Immigration priority is given to those who have a close family relationship with a U.S. citizen or resident, who have needed job skills, are from countries with relatively low levels of immigration to the United States, or who have refugee or asylee status (fleeing his or her own country due to fear of persecution). According to the Office of Immigration Statistics, the majority of new immigrants enter based on family relationship—almost 65 percent in 2008—while the next largest categories

New U.S. citizens recite the pledge of allegiance during a naturalization ceremony in Phoenix, Arizona. More than 1 million people became U.S. citizens in 2008, the largest number in the 100 years the government has been keeping records.

are employment-based, and refugees and asylees, each at about 15 percent. In 2008 1.1 million people became legal permanent residents of the United States, and another million became citizens.

How Immigration Is Changing the U.S. Population

Immigration is the primary source of population growth in the United States, and experts predict that if current immigration trends continue, the percentage of immigrants in the population will increase. Approximately 12 percent of the U.S. population—one in eight—are immigrants. The Pew Research Center projects that the U.S. population will increase from 296 million in 2005 to 438 million in 2050 and that 82 percent of that increase will be due to immigrants and their U.S.-born descendents. The center estimates that by 2050, nearly one in five Americans will be an immigrant. In a July 2008 report for the Federation of American Immigration Reform (FAIR), Jack Martin, director of special projects, reports that between 2000 and 2006 the population increase due to immigration and children born to immigrant mothers was double that of the native-born population. In some states, such as New York and California, he says, immigration actually accounts for all population growth. According to data from the Center for Immigration Studies, California, New York, and New Jersey have the highest percentage of immigrants.

The population of undocumented immigrants in the United States has also increased. The Homeland Security Office of Immigration Statistics estimates that 11.8 million unauthorized immigrants are in the United States, and that this number has increased from 8.5 million in 2000. It reports that 59 percent (7 million) are from Mexico.

As the percentage of immigrants increases, the ethnic composition of the United States is expected to change. According to projections released by the U.S. Census Bureau in August 2008, minorities compose approximately one-third of the U.S. population but by 2050 are expected to be the majority at 54 percent. Hispanic immigrants are the dominant im-

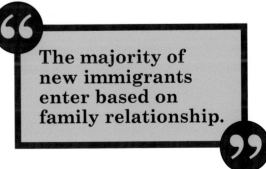

" The majority of new immigrants enter based on family relationship. "

migrant group. The Pew Research Center estimates that Hispanics will increase from 14 percent of the population in 2005 to 29 percent in 2050.

How Does Immigration Affect the Economy?

Disagreement over whether immigration is beneficial or harmful to the economy is widespread. Critics worry that immigration takes jobs away from native-born Americans and drives down wages and that immigrants cause a drain on the economy through remittances and their use of public benefits. Robert E. Rector, senior fellow at the Heritage Foundation, argues, "Current immigration practices, both legal and illegal, operate like a system of transnational welfare outreach bringing millions of fiscally dependent individuals into the U.S."[1] Others insist that immigrants contribute to entrepreneurship and economic growth and fill an important labor need in the United States economy. The *Economist* explains how immigration can be economically beneficial for both home and host countries: "History has shown that immigration encourages prosperity. . . . Many immigrants return home with new skills, savings, technology and bright ideas. . . . It is no coincidence that countries that welcome immigrants—such as Sweden, Ireland, America and Britain—have better economic records than those that shun them."[2]

> " As the percentage of immigrants increases, the ethnic composition of the United States is expected to change. "

How Does Immigration Affect Society?

As a result of the large number of immigrants who come to the United States, immigration has a significant impact on U.S. society. Whether that impact is positive or negative has been the subject of ongoing debate throughout American history. Immigration critics charge that immigration decreases the overall quality of life in the United States, strains education and health care budgets, increases crime, and causes ethnic tensions. Says the Federation for American Immigration Reform, "Estimates of the net cost of immigration run from $30 billion to $50 billion a year. And this is only the quantifiable deficit to local, state, and federal budgets; the deterioration in our quality of life caused by immigration-driven population growth cannot be measured. . . . America's need for immigration ended a century ago."[3]

Immigration advocates contend that not only is immigration not the cause of such social problems but that immigrants actually bring beneficial skills and diversity to the United States. A task force of the Migration Policy Institute insists that immigration has not only benefited the United States in the past but will continue to do so in the future. It says, "Immigration has enabled America's growth and prosperity, and helped shape our dynamic American society. . . . It has been a vital ingredient in America's success. . . . [And] immigration offers the United States unique benefits that will allow us to be a more productive, competitive, and successful nation in the 21st century."[4]

> " Critics worry that immigration takes jobs away from native-born Americans and drives down wages. "

Immigration and Terrorism

Concern about weak immigration laws and lax enforcement of those laws has also prompted worries about a heightened terrorist risk. Following the September 11, 2001, terrorist attacks, focus on this topic has increased. Critics charge that if immigration was better monitored and laws better enforced, the September 11 terrorists would not have been able to stay in the country or carry out their attacks. They argue that immigration needs to be reformed to prevent another attack.

Others argue that stricter immigration enforcement will not eliminate the risk of terrorism. Economist David Friedman maintains that because of the sheer number of people crossing U.S. borders every day, it is impossible for the country to tighten its immigration enforcement to the point where it can prevent terrorists from entering. He says, "In 2004, the most recent year for which I found figures, there were more than eighty million tourist arrivals in North America, presumably most of them in the U.S.

Anyone with sufficient resources and ability to pose a serious terrorist threat can get into the country as one of those tens of millions."[5]

How Should U.S. Immigration Policy Be Reformed?

In June 2009, at a meeting with congressional leaders, President Barack Obama pledged to push aggressively for immigration reform legislation by 2010. The last major change to immigration laws was in 1996, and both lawmakers and the general public express widespread criticism of the current U.S. immigration system and advocate for reform. Areas of immigration that face criticism include the country's inability to prevent millions of undocumented immigrants from entering, U.S. Citizenship and Immigration Services' (USCIS) inefficiency, and current admittance quotas and processes, which many believe are outdated and unrealistic. Senator John McCain of Arizona says, "The simple fact is that America's immigration system is broken."[6] Although the general consensus is that reform is needed, all facets of potential reform are in dispute. Even U.S. Citizenship and Immigration Services agrees that an easy way to reform immigration does not exist. In its Strategic Plan for 2008–2012 the agency says, "The phenomenon of immigration is complex and multifaceted. . . . Assessing impacts and selecting policy options are different even among experts."[7]

> "Immigration advocates contend . . . that immigrants actually bring beneficial skills and diversity to the United States."

Skilled Workers

In 2008 only about 15 percent of immigrants admitted to the United States entered based on job skills. One controversial element of U.S. immigration policy is whether the country should reform its quotas to admit more skilled workers. Many people argue that it should. The National Foundation for American Policy reports that the average high-tech company has 470 openings it cannot fill. Chairman of Microsoft Bill Gates says, "I know we all want the U.S. to continue to be the world's center for innovation. But our position is at risk. . . . U.S. innovation has always been based, in part, on the contributions of foreign-born scientists and researchers. . . . But as you know, our immigration system makes it very difficult for U.S. firms to hire highly skilled foreign workers."[8]

Others contend that plenty of highly skilled U.S. workers are available, but the problem is that companies are not willing to pay them enough because they are able to pay foreign skilled workers lower wages. In one anonymous reply to a *USA Today* editorial a critic writes: "I happen to be an IT hiring manager, and I can assure you that every time we have an opening we are swamped with talent, and we have no positions that stay open for long."[9]

Refugees and Asylum Seekers

Every year, people who are subject to fear or persecution in their own country apply for asylum or refugee status in the United States. This persecution may be due to factors such as race, religion, nationality, or political opinion. Those who apply from outside the country are classified as refugees, and those already inside the United States or at a U.S. port of entry may apply for asylum. The United States accepts a limited number of applicants every year. In 2007, according to the U.S. Department of Homeland Security Office of Immigration Statistics, 48,217 people were admitted as refugees and 25,270 were granted asylum. In 2007 the majority of refugees came from Burma, Somalia, and Iran, while asylum cases were most commonly from China, Colombia, and Haiti. U.S. policy in relation to refugee and asylum seekers is both praised and criticized. Some people charge that the United States does not accept enough refugees and

> Concern about weak immigration laws and lax enforcement of those laws has . . . prompted worries about a heightened terrorist risk.

that those it does accept are often treated poorly. For example, Amnesty International (AI) USA says, "Virtually all asylum seekers apprehended at U.S. borders are subjected to lengthy detention regardless of their individual circumstances. AIUSA calls on immigration officials to release from detention asylum seekers who represent no danger to the community and who are likely to appear at their hearings."[10]

Others disagree, pointing out that the United States settles more refugees than any other country in the world. Says American Enterprise Institute fellow Mauro De Lorenzo, "I often hear refugee advocates complain about unfairness in the U.S. asylum system. From my perspective—comparing it to the situation in developing countries—it looks very different. The American refugee system is the best in the world."[11]

How Should the United States Address the Issue of Illegal Immigration?

An estimated 12 million undocumented immigrants are in the United States, and as a result, a large part of the immigration debate centers on how the country should deal with the issue of illegal immigration. On one side of the debate are those who advocate securing the border and enforcing existing laws. Those such as journalist Fred Reed argue that undocumented immigrants continue to come to the United States because the country does nothing to stop them and even offers attractive advantages for those who do come. He says, "We say to impoverished Mexicans, 'See this river? Don't cross it. If you do, we'll give you good jobs, drivers licenses, citizenship for your kids born here, school for said kids, public assistance. . . . There is no penalty for getting caught. Now, don't cross this river, hear?' How smart is that? . . . Immigrant parents would be irresponsible not to cross."[12] Critics insist that to solve the problem of illegal immigration, the United States needs to secure the border, deport undocumented immigrants, and institute harsh penalties on employers that hire them.

> "Although the general consensus is that reform is needed, all facets of potential reform are in dispute."

On the other side are those people who argue that such an approach is unrealistic. They point out that millions of undocumented immigrants are in the United States and to deport them all would be impossible and undesirable. Instead, they argue, those already in the country should be allowed a path to legalization. In addition, critics insist that to impact

Concerns about illegal immigration bring out protesters on both sides of the issue at a 2006 rally in Framingham, Massachusetts. Similar protests were held on the same weekend in 20 states.

the problem of illegal immigration, the United States needs to do more than simply enforce immigration laws; instead it needs to address the causes of that immigration. The American Civil Liberties Union argues that increased border enforcement has not stopped undocumented immigration because the forces pushing people to migrate, such as poverty or lack of freedom in their own countries, are stronger than the challenge of crossing the border.

Recent Increase in Immigration Enforcement

While no new immigration legislation has been passed by Congress in recent years, a recent surge in U.S. immigration enforcement has occurred. Funding for the federal agencies that enforce immigration laws has increased greatly, and both border and interior enforcement have increased. The budget for U.S. Customs and Border Protection (CBP), the parent agency of the Border Patrol within the Department of Homeland Security (DHS), increased from $6 billion in 2004 to $9.3 billion in 2008.

> U.S. policy in relation to refugee and asylum seekers is both praised and criticized.

The budget of U.S. Immigration and Customs Enforcement (ICE), the DHS interior-enforcement counterpart to CBP, increased from $3.7 billion in 2004 to $5.1 billion in 2008. Miles of border fencing, the number of border patrol agents, and detention beds to hold illegal aliens have all increased significantly.

DHS reports that between 2007 and 2008 apprehensions of undocumented immigrants in the United States increased by 27 percent. Work site raids in which unauthorized workers are apprehended and removed from the country have also increased. For example, April 2008 raids of chicken-processing plants in Texas, Florida, Tennessee, Arkansas, and West Virginia led to the arrest of more than 280 workers, and December 2006 raids of meat-processing plants in Colorado, Nebraska, Texas, Utah, Iowa, and Minnesota resulted in 1,297 arrests.

In addition to increased enforcement, the level of state action regarding immigration has been unprecedented. As the National Conference of State Legislatures (NCSL) explains, a lack of federal immigration reform has forced states to act instead:

> As the immigration reform debate has intensified at the federal level, states have been left to grapple with the adverse effects of immigration. . . . Immigration issues have gained in prominence in state legislatures across the country. As the federal government has faced gridlock in reforming legal and illegal immigration, states have looked for mechanisms to respond to the public's concerns.[13]

According to NCSL, in 2007 every state considered immigration legislation. In 2008, 206 state immigration laws were enacted. State immigration laws have been primarily focused on employment, identification/driver's licenses, and law enforcement. A number of laws concerning the access of undocumented immigrants to public services have also been enacted.

An Issue of Vital Importance

In the United States people continue to debate how immigration affects the economy and society, how immigration policy should be reformed, and how the country should deal with the issue of illegal immigration. As Robert J. Sampson, chair of the Sociology Department at Harvard University points out, this is a vitally important issue for the United States. He says, "Although Americans hold polarizing and conflicting views about its values, immigration is a major social force that will continue for some time."[14]

How Does Immigration Affect the Economy?

66Natives and migrants alike gain [from immigration] as larger workforces speed up economic growth; and . . . foreigners not only fill jobs but act as entrepreneurs who in turn create jobs and wealth.99

—*The Economist*, weekly newspaper.

66No American wage earner benefits from having his or her elected officials import workers [through immigration].99

—Smart Business Practices, pro-business resource for American businesspeople.

I n a study of the effect of immigration policy on the economy, the economic analysis firm the Perryman Group estimates that one in eight people living in the United States is an immigrant. As this figure makes clear, immigrants are an important part of the U.S. economy and have a significant impact on it. Of particular concern are immigration's effect on American jobs and wages, immigrant use of public benefits, and the impact of immigrant remittances and entrepreneurship. Also discussed is the effect of illegal immigrants in terms of taxes and worker exploitation.

One common critique of immigration is that immigrants drive down the wages of native-born Americans. Steven A. Camarota, research director for the Center for Immigration Studies, has examined U.S. employment data between 2000 and 2004 and theorizes that immigrants may be taking jobs from native-born Americans. During that time, he found, unemployment increased among native-born Americans while the number of immigrants holding jobs increased. "It would be a mistake to think that every job taken by an immigrant is a job lost by a native," says Camarota, "but it would also be a mistake to assume that dramatically increasing the number of [immigrant] workers . . . has no impact on the employment prospects of some natives."[15]

> One common critique of immigration is that immigrants drive down the wages of native-born Americans.

Others insist that immigrants do not take American jobs. In the opinion of Raymond Keating, chief economist for the Small Business and Entrepreneurship Council, data on the U.S. workforce shows that "immigrants are not crowding out workers, but simply meeting the need for more labor."[16] A study by Michael Porter of the Harvard Business School found that immigrants who live in inner cities actually cause economic growth and create jobs. In an analysis of job growth between 1995 and 2003, he found that city populations with a high percentage of immigrants created a higher number of jobs than those with a low percentage of immigrants. The study showed that on average, inner cities that gained jobs had populations that were 31 percent immigrant, while those that lost jobs had populations that were just 12 percent immigrant.

Undocumented Immigrants and American Jobs

The impact of undocumented immigrants on jobs is a particularly controversial issue. Many people charge that undocumented immigrants pose a particular threat to the economy because they depress wages and take jobs away from natives and legal residents. In a 2008 study of undocumented immigrants in Arizona, George J. Borjas, professor of economics and social policy at the Kennedy School of Government, Harvard University, found that these workers increase the number of available workers in the state and drive down wages. He reports that undocumented immigrants cost Arizonans at least $1.4 billion in lower wages in 2005.

Critics contend that undocumented immigrants are an important source of labor in industries that need large numbers of low-skilled workers such as agriculture, construction, and some service and manufacturing industries. Judith Gans of the University of Arizona, key author of a 2007 study about the impact of undocumented immigrants in Arizona, argues, "Because [undocumented] immigrants are filling specific gaps in Arizona's labor force, they are making possible economic activity that otherwise would not occur."[17] According to Gans, eliminating undocumented workers would result in lost economic output of approximately $29 billion each year for Arizona.

> " **Immigrants to the United States are eligible for various public benefits.** "

Public Benefits

Immigrants to the United States are eligible for various public benefits, and the economic impact of immigrants' use of such benefits is the focus of fierce debate. Some research shows that immigrants are more likely to be poor and uneducated and to use public benefits, and thus many people charge that they harm the economy by causing a financial drain. Explain Edwin Meese III and Matthew Spalding of the Heritage Foundation,

> While the government continues its massive efforts to reduce overall poverty, immigration policy in the United States tends to produce results in the opposite direction, increasing rather than decreasing the poverty problem. Immigrants with low skill levels have a high probability of poverty and of receiving benefits and services that drive up governmental welfare, health, social service, and education costs."[18]

In a 2008 report the Perryman Group finds that 33 percent of immigrant households use a major welfare program, compared with only 19 percent of native-born families. In a 2007 Center for Immigration Studies report, Camarota cites a number of statistics showing a higher incidence of poverty among and use of public benefits by immigrants than among and by the native born in the United States. For example, he says that 34 percent of immigrants do not have health insurance, compared with 13 percent of natives, meaning that they will be more likely to use public benefits. While immigrants do make progress over time, he says, even 20 years after coming to the United States they are more likely than natives to be poor, use welfare, or lack insurance.

Others insist that immigrants do not take more from the government than they contribute. The Immigration Policy Center points out that even though they pay taxes, immigrants are restricted from receiving most federal benefits for the first five years they are in the country. According to a 2008 report by the American Civil Liberties Union, immigrants use medical services less than the average American and are also less likely to use food stamps. Columnist Jason L. Riley maintains that while it is a popular belief that immigrants use more public benefits than the native born, the facts do not support this. He says, "It turns out that low-income immigrants who qualify for public benefits sign up at much lower rates than low-income natives."[19]

Entrepreneurship

People disagree over whether immigrants benefit the country more than the native born in terms of entrepreneurship. Entrepreneurs benefit the economy by creating jobs and wealth, and some people insist that immigrants are more likely to bring the ideas and the desire to take risks that lead to such entrepreneurship. Says Keating, "Only true risk takers leave behind their home country to pursue dreams in another nation. Such people built America and more come and make valuable contributions today."[20] According to an index of entrepreneurial activity by the Kaufman Foundation, an organization devoted to entrepreneurship, in 2005 the rate of entrepreneurial activity for immigrants was 0.35 percent, while it was only 0.28 percent for native-born Americans.

> **People disagree over whether immigrants benefit the country more than the native born in terms of entrepreneurship.**

However, other research shows that immigrants may actually have a lower rate of entrepreneurship. According to Mark Krikorian, head of the Center for Immigration Studies and author of *The New Case Against Immigration*, Mexicans, the largest immigrant group to the United States, have one of the lowest rates of entrepreneurship—significantly lower than that of the native born.

Remittances

Many immigrants to the United States send remittances to their home countries. While most agree that these remittances are beneficial to the home countries because they provide income and stability to the people there, some debate the impact such remittances have on the U.S. economy. Banco de Mexico reports that in 2006 Mexicans sent approximately $23 billion home in remittances. The American Civil Liberties Union reports that 51 percent of Latino immigrants—the largest immigrant group in the United States—send remittances home.

Researchers debate whether remittances are harmful or beneficial to the United States economy. Critics argue that the economy is harmed by this high rate of remittances because billions of dollars are being sent to other countries instead of being spent in the United States. Others argue that while many immigrants do send remittances home, they also spend large amounts of money in the United States on goods and services, taxes, and Social Security.

> In 2006 Mexicans sent approximately $23 billion home in remittances.

They also argue that remittances actually benefit the United States because they make it possible for more poor people to stay in their home countries rather than migrate to the United States. Finally, remittances benefit the U.S. economy through the billions of dollars in bank fees that U.S. banks receive for these international money transfers.

Taxes and Government Benefits for Undocumented Immigrants

Most undocumented immigrants pay some form of tax; however, how much is paid and whether it is more or less than what is received in government benefits is a subject of debate. The Media Matters Action Network describes the ways that undocumented immigrants pay taxes:

Undocumented immigrants pay all kinds of taxes: they pay sales taxes whenever they purchase goods and services, they pay property taxes in the form of rent, and they pay payroll and income taxes. Many undocumented immigrants use false Social Security numbers to obtain employment; when they do so, these workers then pay payroll taxes (for Social Security and Medicare), and often federal and state income taxes as well. [21]

In a 2005 article the *New York Times* estimated that in 2002 undocumented immigrants paid $6.4 billion in Social Security taxes. While undocumented immigrants pay all these taxes, they are not eligible for most government benefits, such as Social Security, so many people argue that the net effect is positive for the U.S. economy.

However, others argue that despite the taxes they pay, undocumented immigrants have a negative effect overall. While they are unable to receive most public benefits, undocumented immigrants do receive some. Colum-

> Most of the taxes paid by undocumented immigrants go to the federal government, while the public services immigrants use are paid for by the state.

nist Thomas Sowell argues that these benefits are costly. He says, "[Undocumented immigrants] are no bargain for taxpayers who cover their medical bills, the education of their children and the costs of imprisoning those who commit a disproportionate share of crime."[22] Others point out that most of the taxes paid by undocumented immigrants go to the federal government, while the public services immigrants use are paid for by the state. Because of the way taxes are distributed, certain local entities such as schools and hospitals may spend money on undocumented workers that they do not receive back in taxes.

Illegal Immigration and Workplace Exploitation
Many people believe that when large numbers of undocumented immigrants come to the United States for work, this leads to workplace exploi-

tation which lowers the quality of working conditions for all workers. Because they are not legally allowed to work, undocumented workers must accept whatever wages or conditions they are offered by employers. In addition, most undocumented immigrants are afraid to complain about dangerous or illegal workplace conditions for fear of being deported. Tiberio Chavez, an undocumented worker from Mexico, talks about his first job in a meatpacking plant in Omaha, Nebraska. He says, "It was a cold, dirty, tough job, and poorly paid. . . . The job started at four in the morning and ended at six or seven in the evening, for $3.50 an hour. Since I wanted to work, I was ready to deal with those things."[23]

Rinku Sen, president and executive director of the Applied Research Center and publisher of *ColorLines*, and Moroccan immigrant Fekkak Mamdouh explain that the level of working conditions for all workers is lowered when undocumented immigrants accept whatever conditions they are offered. They maintain, "When undocumented people cannot protect their rights, employers are able to abuse them, which . . . drives down working conditions for everyone else. . . . [And] immigrants who are driven underground out of fear become vulnerable to all kinds of crime, undermining the rule of law rather than strengthening it."[24]

Stephen Steinlight, senior policy analyst at the Center for Immigration Studies, gives the example of the May 2008 Immigration and Customs Enforcement Agency raid of the AgriProcessors meat processing plant in Iowa to show the correlation between the presence of undocumented workers and illegal workplace conduct. Not only were 389 illegal aliens arrested, he says, but the attorney general of the state of Iowa indicted the company, managers, and owners on numerous counts of violating state child labor laws.

A Significant Impact

Immigrants make up a significant percentage of the American population, and as a result they also play a significant role in the country's economy. Debate about whether that role is positive or negative is widespread, and numerous studies exist to support both sides of the debate. However, despite such debate the fact remains that immigrants are an influential and integral part of America's economy.

Primary Source Quotes*

How Does Immigration Affect the Economy?

❝Immigrants provide tremendous benefits to our economy.❞

—Raymond Keating, "Commentary: Before Reform, Know the Good Side of Immigration," *Long Island Business News*, May 23, 2008.

Keating is chief economist for the Small Business & Entrepreneurship Council.

❝On balance, current mass immigration contributes essentially nothing [economically] to native-born Americans.❞

—Peter Brimelow, "Economics of Immigration and the Course of the Debate Since 1994," in Carol M. Swain, ed., *Debating Immigration*. New York: Cambridge University Press, 2007.

Brimelow is a senior fellow at the Pacific Research Institute and a columnist for *CBS MarketWatch*.

Bracketed quotes indicate conflicting positions.

* Editor's Note: While the definition of a primary source can be narrowly or broadly defined, for the purposes of Compact Research, a primary source consists of: 1) results of original research presented by an organization or researcher; 2) eyewitness accounts of events, personal experience, or work experience; 3) first-person editorials offering pundits' opinions; 4) government officials presenting political plans and/or policies; 5) representatives of organizations presenting testimony or policy.

❝Whether we are here legally or illegally, we are still paying taxes. We pay our bills. Most of the money we make stays here in payments. . . . No one should look down on us, because we are helping the country.❞

—Lorenzo Francisco, "My Children Need My Presence," in David Bacon, *Communities Without Borders: Images and Voices from the World of Migration.* Ithaca, NY: Cornell University Press, 2006.

Francisco is an undocumented immigrant from Guatemala. He works in Omaha, Nebraska, to support his wife and seven children who live back in Guatemala.

❝Illegal immigration is not a victimless crime. . . . It causes an enormous drain on public services, depresses wages of American workers, contributes to population growth that, in turn, contributes to school overcrowding and housing shortages. . . . Directly and indirectly, U.S. taxpayers are paying for illegal immigration.❞

—American Legion, "The American Legion Policy on Illegal Immigration: A Strategy to Address Illegal Immigration in the United States," 2008. www.legion.org.

The American Legion is a nonprofit wartime veterans organization. It has approximately 3 million members worldwide.

❝Immigration policy in the United States . . . [is] increasing rather than decreasing the poverty problem. Immigrants with low skill levels have a high probability of poverty and of receiving benefits and services that drive up governmental welfare, health, social service, and education costs.❞

—Edwin Meese III and Matthew Spalding, "Where We Stand: Essential Requirements for Immigration Reform," *Backgrounder,* no. 2034, Heritage Foundation, May 10, 2007.

Meese is a Ronald Reagan Distinguished Fellow in Public Policy and chairman of the Center for Legal and Judicial Studies, and Spalding is director of the B. Kenneth Simon Center for American Studies at the Heritage Foundation.

66On average, US natives benefit from immigration. Immigrants tend to complement (not substitute for) natives, raising natives' productivity and income.99

—Council of Economic Advisers, "Immigration's Economic Impact," Executive Office of the President, June 20, 2007. www.whitehouse.gov.

The Council of Economic Advisers is a group of economists who advise the U.S. president.

66There is evidence that immigration is adversely impacting employment of native-born workers. . . . [Data between 2000 and 2004 show that] the number of immigrants with jobs increased dramatically at the same time as the number of unemployed natives looking for jobs also increased.99

—Steven A. Camarota, "Immigrant Employment Gains and Native Losses, 2000–2004," in Carol M. Swain, ed., *Debating Immigration*. New York: Cambridge University Press, 2007.

Camarota is research director at the Center for Immigration Studies.

66By paying taxes and Social Security, immigrants contribute far more to government coffers that they use in social services.99

—American Civil Liberties Union, "Immigration Myths and Facts—January 2008," January 25, 2008. www.aclu.org.

The American Civil Liberties Union is an organization that works to preserve the indivdual rights and freedoms guaranteed by the Costitution and the laws of the United States.

How Does Immigration Affect the Economy?

- According to a 2007 report by the Council of Economic Advisers, in 2006 approximately **15 percent** of the U.S. labor force was composed of foreign-born workers.

- A 2007 Heritage Foundation study found that in 2004 low-wage immigrant families caused a net fiscal deficit of **$89.1 billion**.

- In 2007 Los Angeles County reported that illegal immigration cost the county **$220 million** for safety, **$400 million** for health care, and **$440 million** for welfare each year.

- According to a 2008 *USA Today* report, an estimated **three-quarters** of illegal workers pay taxes that contribute to Social Security and Medicare.

- The Center for Immigration Studies reports that in 2007, **31 percent** of adult immigrants had not completed high school, compared with **8 percent** of natives.

- According to the *Washington Post* in 2008, **one in five** college-educated immigrants is unemployed or working in an unskilled job.

- Mexico's central bank reports that in 2007 immigrants working in the United States sent **$26 billion** home in remittances.

Biggest Immigration Concern Is Jobs

Many people believe that immigrants lower the wages of American workers and take jobs from them. According to the results of this poll conducted by the Pew Research Center, the impact of immigrants on jobs is a major concern. The poll finds that among those people who believe that immigration laws need to be changed, the biggest concern is that immigration hurts American jobs.

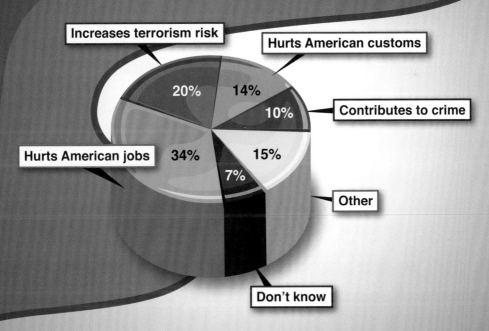

Source: Pew Research Center for the People & the Press, "Democratic Leaders Face Growing Disapproval, Criticism on Iraq: Mixed Views on Immigration Bill," June 7, 2007. www.people-press.org.

- The *San Francisco Chronicle* reports that money transfer companies and banks charge an average of **6 percent** for immigrant remittance transfers.

- The *Wall Street Journal* reports that in 2008 the amount of money sent home by Mexicans working in the United States declined by **3.6 percent**, the first decline in 13 years.

Increasing Remittances to Mexico

According to this chart of remittances to Mexico, the amount of money sent from the United States to Mexico—for example from immigrant workers to families back home—increased steadily from 1996 to 2006, and has stayed at high levels since then. There is disagreement over whether or not remittances harm the United States economy.

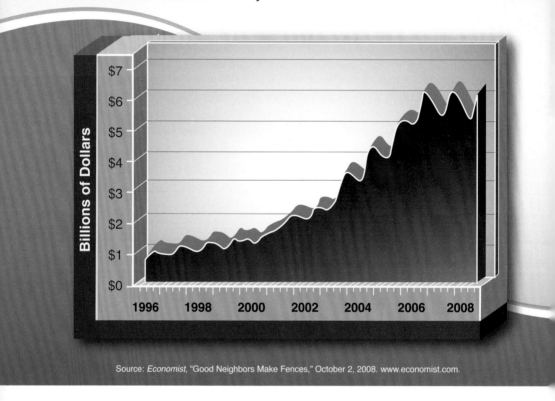

Source: *Economist*, "Good Neighbors Make Fences," October 2, 2008. www.economist.com.

- A June/July 2008 Gallup poll of 1,900 adult Americans nationwide found that by **a 2-to-1** margin, respondents believed that immigrants cost taxpayers too much in terms of their use of government services versus the taxes they pay.

How Does Immigration Affect Society?

66 **The overriding impact of immigrants is to strengthen and enrich American culture . . . and raise the standard of living of American citizens.** 99

—Center for Trade Policy Studies, Cato Institute.

66 **Today's level of immigration is simply too high to be . . . consistent with U.S. national needs and priorities.** 99

—Federation for American Immigration Reform, national nonprofit immigration reform organization.

Because of the sheer number of people who immigrate—legally and illegally—to the United States, immigration has a significant impact on society. Widespread debate continues over how it is changing the population and its quality of life, and how it impacts crime, national security, education, and health care. People also disagree over how immigration is related to the spread of disease and over the rate of immigrant assimilation.

Changing Population

Immigrants are a large and continually increasing percentage of the U.S. population and are changing its ethnic composition. According to Jeffrey S. Passel and D'Vera Cohn of the Pew Research Center, "Nearly all of the [projected population] increase from 2005 to 2050 will be due to new immigrants and their U.S.-born descendents. They will account for 82% of the nation's population growth."[25] The center estimates that by 2050, almost 1 in 5 Americans will be an immigrant, compared to 1 in 8 in 2005. Because so much of America's future population growth will be due to immigrants, the nation's racial and ethnic mix is expected to change. The biggest change is that the Hispanic population is expected to increase from 14 percent of the population in 2005 to 29 percent in 2050. The Pew Research Center projects that the non-Hispanic white population will become a minority by 2050.

> **Immigrants are a large and continually increasing percentage of the U.S. population.**

Professor of sociology Lingxin Hao at Johns Hopkins University stresses that these immigration-based population changes will have a significant impact on society. He says, "Immigration accounts for 60 percent of U.S. population growth. . . . Such a large-scale, ongoing population change can profoundly interfere with the social structure and social processes of a society."[26]

Quality of Life

Some people believe that current levels of immigration are decreasing the quality of life in the United States because as the population grows it has to compete for scarce natural resources. Mark Krikorian, head of the Center for Immigration Studies and author of *The New Case Against Immigration*, says, "[Immigration] is undermining a variety of modern goals related to quality of life, including cleaner air and water, reduced congestion, and the preservation of our nation's natural beauty and historic inheritance."[27] Jack Martin, director of special projects for the Federation for American Immigration Reform, agrees. He believes that the United States cannot sustain an infinitely increasing number of people, warning, "Our population already significantly exceeds the carrying capacity of our land. . . . If . . . our population continues to grow, our dependence on other lands to support us will necessarily also increase."[28]

Others contend that such assertions are false. Argues *Wall Street Journal* columnist Jason L. Riley, "The United States is nowhere close to being overpopulated. America is a very large country, and the vast majority of it remains quite empty."[29] In addition, says Riley, at the same time as the U.S. population has increased, environmental quality has improved, natural resources have increased, and the quality of life has actually improved. Riley and others contend that immigration is actually beneficial because it spurs research and development that improves the quality of life in the United States.

Crime

People disagree over how immigration impacts crime in the United States. Numerous polls show that a significant percentage of the population believes that immigration increases crime. For example, according to a 2007 survey by the Pew Research Center, the fear that immigration contributes to crime ranked as the third biggest immigration-related concern among respondents. However, the data does not back up this belief about a correlation between immigration and crime. For example, statistics show that since the 1990s, immigration to the United States has increased, while the general level of crime has decreased. Critics point out that immigrants actually have good reason not to be involved in crime. The Immigration Policy Center argues, "Immigrants . . . come to build better lives for themselves and their families. As a result, they have little to gain and much to lose by breaking the law."[30] Critics also point out that immigrants are screened for criminal activity before they are allowed permanent residency, so the incidence of crime by immigrants is likely to be lower.

> **Some people believe that current levels of immigration are decreasing the quality of life in the United States.**

The relationship between undocumented immigrants and crime is a particularly controversial subject. In a 2007 report FAIR found that illegal aliens are more likely to be incarcerated than the rest of the population. FAIR explains why it believes this is so: "Those who sneak into the country undergo no form of screening for criminality or any other grounds for exclusion. Many . . . end up incarcerated as a result of criminal activity at the time of their illegal entry. . . . Other illegal aliens owe alien smugglers for assisting in their illegal entry and end up being co-opted into criminal activity . . . to pay off the debt."[31] The Immigration Policy Center disagrees, pointing out that while the undocumented immigrant population doubled between 1994 and 2004, the violent crime rate decreased 35.1 percent, and the property crime rate fell by 25 percent.

Concerns About Immigration and Threats to National Security

Many fear that by not reforming and properly enforcing its immigration laws, the United States faces a significant national security risk. The biggest critique is that if large numbers of undocumented immigrants can enter the United States, then it might be possible for potential terrorists to do the same thing. In *Whatever It Takes*, Congressman J.D. Hayworth points out how easy it would be for a terrorist to illegally enter the United States through its border with Mexico in the same way that other undocumented immigrants enter. He says, "At least three illegals make it across the border for every one who is caught. . . . Keep in mind that it takes only a handful of committed terrorists to strike a devastating blow."[32] Krikorian believes that simply too many people—illegal and legal—are entering the United States for the country to successfully stop potential terrorists from entering. He says, "Overwhelmed inspectors are simply unable to do their jobs properly."[33]

> **People disagree over how immigration impacts crime in the United States.**

However, critics argue that despite fears that lax immigration enforcement increases the terrorist risk, no evidence shows a correlation between immigration and terrorism. For example, an examination of the September 11, 2001, hijackers reveals that while some had fallen out of legal immigration status at the time of the attacks, they did not sneak into the country; instead, they all entered legally. Say Sen and Mamdouh, "There has been no sign that restricting immigration will have any effect on preventing terrorism."[34]

Education

Some critics charge that immigration has a negative impact on education because it increases overall costs. Krikorian explains how: First, he says, immigrants are likely to have more school-age children than are native-born people, which increases the total number of children whom the state must pay to educate. In addition, he says, many immigrant children have limited English proficiency, which adds to the cost of their education. The Federation for American Immigration Reform argues that a limited amount of money is available for education in the United States and that the native born suffer when that money is used to pay for the education of immigrants. It says,

> Rather than being used to improve the quality of education for current students, communities' limited tax dollars are instead being diverted to build new schools to accommodate population growth and to meet the special needs of immigrant children. Including special programs such as bilingual education, which can cost nearly 50 percent more than regular schooling, immigration costs the taxpayers over $24 billion a year in education costs.[35]

Others argue that while immigration may increase education costs, the benefits of immigrants to the United States outweigh the negative impact of these costs. The American Civil Liberties Union agrees that states pay a high cost in educating the children of immigrants but believes that when the overall economic benefits of immigration are considered, such as immigrants' role in sustaining local economies, the overall impact is positive. In addition is the argument that educated immigrants make greater economic and social contributions to the United States than uneducated ones.

Health Care

Many immigrants do not have health insurance, and critics charge that when these uninsured immigrants need medical care and are unable to pay for it, taxpayers are forced to pay the bill. According to Krikorian, approximately one in three immigrants in the United States does not have health insurance. He explains how this can impose a significant cost on consumers and the government. Says Krikorian, "Even the uninsured get sick, and no modern society is going to allow them to go entirely without treatment."[36] Most uninsured immigrants who need medical care get it at emergency rooms. Emergency rooms are required by law to screen and stabilize anyone who comes for medical treatment, whether the sick person can afford it or not. Krikorian quotes statistics from California and Texas, which have high immigrant populations, to show that emergency room use by uninsured immigrants poses a significant cost for the state. He says that in California, where the majority of the uninsured are immigrants, emergency departments lost almost half a billion dollars in 2001–2002; and in Texas, where 4 in 10 of the uninsured are immigrants, the state's trauma centers lost $181 million in 2001.

> Some critics charge that immigration has a negative impact on education because it increases overall costs.

Not everyone agrees that uninsured immigrants impose high costs on U.S. society. Some argue that while immigrants might be statistically likely to be uninsured, they are also more likely to be younger and healthier than natives and thus less likely to incur large bills for medical care. Some people argue that U.S. health care problems are not the fault of immigrants but of other social factors. For example, professor of U.S. history and Chicano studies Justin Akers Chacón agrees that America's health care system is strained, but he believes this has nothing to do with immigrants. He argues that the United States simply has a health care crisis. "Social spending *for all workers* has been drastically cut or reduced in the last decades," says Chacón. "About 46 million working people do not have access to health care."[37]

Undocumented Immigration and Disease

Some people believe that undocumented immigrants bring new and harmful diseases to the United States from other countries. In his book *Whatever It Takes*, Hayworth explains the possible connection between undocumented immigration and disease. He says, "Since illegal aliens are not screened for diseases, they can walk in with . . . drug-resistant tuberculosis (which can cost up to $1 million to treat), Chagas, acute hepatitis, chronic hepatitis C, and sexually transmitted diseases."[38] The United States has seen an increase in some of these diseases, such as drug-resistant tuberculosis; however, critics insist that the assertion that this increase is due to immigrants has not been proved, and conclusive research on this topic is lacking.

Some people argue that in many cases, the opposite is actually true—immigrants contract various illnesses and diseases from people in the United States. As a result of his research on migrant workers, Chacón maintains, "Far from being the 'harbingers of disease' that anti-immigrant demagogues decry . . . migrant workers are largely the victims of ailments and disease that they contract *while working in the United States*."[39]

Assimilation

The degree to which immigrants are currently assimilating in the United States is also debated. Critics charge that many are not assimilating, which causes racial tension between various ethnicities and cultures and threatens the social cohesion of communities. Krikorian explains why assimilation might not be happening or might be slower than in the past. He says, "Modern technology now enables newcomers to retain ties to their homelands . . . thus, becoming 'deeply rooted here,' . . . is simply less likely to happen."[40]

Many immigrants do retain strong ties with their homelands; for example, even when they become U.S. citizens many people do not give up their previous citizenship, holding dual citizenship instead. While people debate whether immigrants are assimilating in a way that benefits themselves or U.S. society, evidence suggests that some assimilation is occurring. For example, record numbers of immigrants are applying for U.S. citizenship—an important part of assimilation—even though it is an expensive and difficult process. In a 2007 report the Pew Hispanic Center finds that the children of Hispanic immigrants are becoming proficient in English, another part of assimilation. It reports

> " Many immigrants do retain strong ties with their homelands . . . even when they become U.S. citizens. "

that 91 percent of second-generation Hispanics can speak English well, and 97 percent of third-generation Hispanics can.

A Major Social Force

Widespread debate continues over exactly how immigrants affect life in the United States. As professor of demographic studies Charles F. Westoff points out, though, "However one evaluates the net costs and benefits of immigration, it is a major demographic force . . . in the United States."[41]

Primary Source Quotes*

How Does Immigration Affect Society?

66 In town after town throughout the U.S., communities are finding that today's rapid population growth is overcrowding schools, clogging roads, swallowing up open space, taxing the environment, and raising the cost of living for all. It is difficult to imagine the consequences if policy makers continue to ignore the problem of high-level immigration. 99

—Jack Martin, "Immigration and U.S. Population Growth," Federation for American Immigration Reform, July 2008. www.fairus.org.

Martin is director of special projects at the Federation for American Immigration Reform.

66 [Despite the fact that] a new immigrant arrives every 30 seconds . . . we 300 million Americans are on balance healthier and wealthier and freer than . . . ever: We breathe cleaner air, drink cleaner water, earn higher incomes, have more leisure time, and live in less crowded housing. 99

—Stephen Moore, "300,000,000," *Wall Street Journal*, October 3, 2006. www.wsj.com.

Moore is a member of the *Wall Street Journal*'s editorial board.

Bracketed quotes indicate conflicting positions.

* Editor's Note: While the definition of a primary source can be narrowly or broadly defined, for the purposes of Compact Research, a primary source consists of: 1) results of original research presented by an organization or researcher; 2) eyewitness accounts of events, personal experience, or work experience; 3) first-person editorials offering pundits' opinions; 4) government officials presenting political plans and/or policies; 5) representatives of organizations presenting testimony or policy.

Primary Source Quotes

"Immigrants . . . are mostly young, fit and hard-working. They do not come with the express purpose of seeking free health care. . . . There are numerous indications that immigrants . . . use less health care and are more likely to pay for it than America's own native poor."

—Zagreus Ammon, "Immigration and Health Care Costs," Physician Executive, January 4, 2008. http://executivephysician.blogspot.com.

Zagreus Ammon is the pen name of a physician who writes a blog about health care and medicine. The author is a fellow of the American Academy of Family Physicians and of the College of Family Physicians of Canada.

"One in four people in the United States without health insurance is an immigrant. . . . Immigrants without any insurance at all . . . impose significant costs on government and on consumers."

—Mark Krikorian, *The New Case Against Immigration: Both Legal and Illegal*. New York: Sentinel, 2008.

Krikorian is executive director of the Center for Immigration Studies and a regular contributor to the *National Review*.

"As of 2007 there was no documented basis for any suggested link of terrorism with Mexico or with movement across the U.S.-Mexico boundary."

—Joseph Nevins, *Dying to Live*. San Francisco: Open Media/City Lights, 2008.

Nevins is the author of *Dying to Live*.

"Terrorists know all about our contradictory immigration policies. They have taken advantage of them before, and there is no reason to think they will not do so again. We ignore that fact at our own peril."

—J.D. Hayworth, with Joseph J. Eule, *Whatever It Takes: Illegal Immigration, Border Security, and the War on Terror*. Washington, DC: Regnery, 2006.

Hayworth is a former U.S. congressman and is the host of a Phoenix-based radio talk show.

66 Research and experience have shown that today's immigrants integrate into American society just like generations of immigrants before them. **99**

—Immigration Policy Center, "Record-Breaking Number of Immigrants Seek Integration, U.S. Citizenship," September 16, 2008. www.immigrationpolicy.org.

The Immigration Policy Center is the research arm of the American Immigration Law Foundation. Its mission is to provide accurate information about the economic and social effects of immigration in the United States.

66 Immigrants arrive . . . so fast and so many, that they are not assimilating into the American Dream. **99**

—Frosty Wooldridge, "How to Destroy America—Part 2," rense.com, April 17, 2006. www.rense.com.

Wooldridge is a journalist.

Facts and Illustrations

How Does Immigration Affect Society?

- The U.S. Census Bureau estimates that in 2050 the minority population is expected to be **235.7 million** out of a total population of 439 million.

- According to a September 2006 poll of 1,000 likely American voters, commissioned by the Center for Immigration Studies, **40 percent** of those polled strongly agreed, and **26 percent** somewhat agreed, that population growth caused by current immigration policies will lead to increased congestion, overcrowding, and pollution.

- A 2008 Gallup poll finds that **64 percent** of Americans say immigration benefits the United States.

- According to the Immigration Policy Center, while immigration increased between 1994 and 2005, the violent crime rate declined **34.2 percent**, and the property crime rate declined **26.4 percent**.

- Of **1,157 illegal immigrants** arrested during an Immigration and Customs Enforcement Agency sweep in California, **345 had prior criminal convictions**, the *Los Angeles Times* reported.

- According to a 2009 study by the Immigration Reform Coalition of Texas, undocumented immigration costs the state **$4.5 billion** to **$6 billion** a year, primarily in education costs.

Foreign-Born Residents by State

Immigrants compose a large percentage of the U.S. population and have a substantial impact on American culture. This map shows the number of foreign-born individuals by state, based on 2006 statistics. The most foreign-born residents live in California, Texas, Florida, Illinois, New York, and New Jersey.

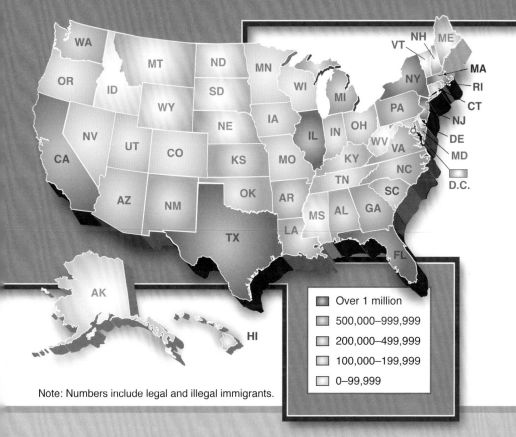

Note: Numbers include legal and illegal immigrants.

Legend:
- Over 1 million
- 500,000–999,999
- 200,000–499,999
- 100,000–199,999
- 0–99,999

Source: Alan Greenblatt, "Immigration Debate," *CQ Researcher*, February 1, 2008, p. 100.

- The Pew Hispanic Center estimates that the children of undocumented immigrants account for **6.8 percent** of the students enrolled in the nation's elementary and secondary schools.

Percentage of Ethnic Minorities in the United States Is Increasing

These graphs show how the ethnic composition of the United States changed between 1970 and 2000, and how it is estimated to change by 2050. The white, non-Hispanic population is decreasing, while the population of Hispanic and other (non-Black) ethnic groups is growing.

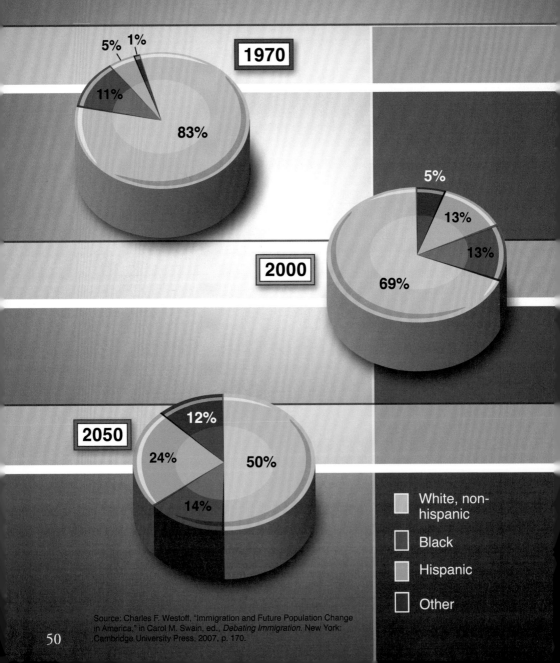

1970

5% 1%
11%
83%

2000

5%
13%
13%
69%

2050

12%
24%
50%
14%

White, non-hispanic

Black

Hispanic

Other

Source: Charles F. Westoff, "Immigration and Future Population Change in America," in Carol M. Swain, ed., *Debating Immigration*. New York: Cambridge University Press, 2007. p. 170.

Homicides Decrease as Immigration Increases

According to this graph, which compares the homicide rate and the immigration rate, increases in immigration do not appear to cause increases in the homicide rate. While the immigration rate increased significantly during the 1990s, the homicide rate decreased significantly.

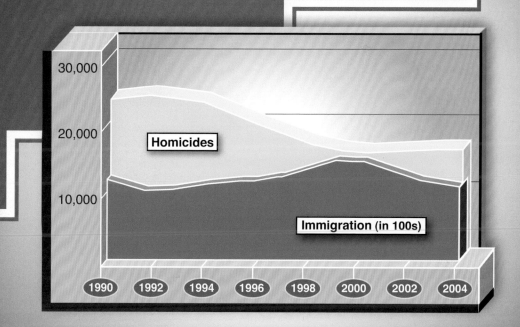

Source: Robert J. Sampson, "Rethinking Crime and Immigration," *Contexts*, Winter 2008, p. 29.

- A 2008 report by the Kaiser Family Foundation found that **78 percent** of those people who did not have medical insurance in 2006 were American citizens.

- According to a 2008 study by the Employee Benefit Research Institute, between 1994 and 2006 immigration accounted for **55 percent** of the increase in the uninsured.

Illegal Aliens Represent a High Share of the Prison Population

This graph compares the percentage of illegal aliens in the prison population with the percentage of illegal aliens in the overall adult population, in eight states. It reveals that in each of these states, illegal aliens represent a disproportionately high share of the prison population.

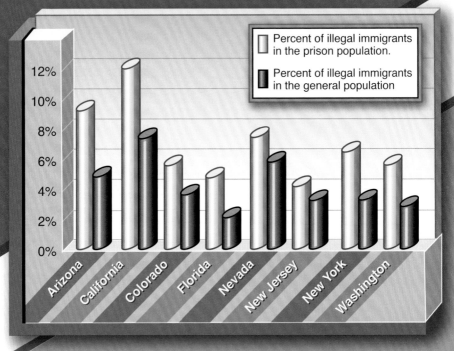

Source: Jack Martin, "Illegal Aliens and Crime Incidence," *Federation for American Immigration Reform*, March 2007. www.fairus.org.

- According to the Migration Policy Institute, **52.4 percent** of America's foreign-born population was limited in English proficiency in 2006.

How Should U.S. Immigration Policy Be Reformed?

66 Only through a comprehensive approach combining reform of our admission system, a realistic solution for the undocumented population . . . and . . . effective enforcement of realistic laws will we gain control over our immigration system. 99

—National Immigration Forum, pro-immigration organization.

66 As we struggle with this issue . . . it is clear that we have come to no generally accepted and politically realizable conclusions as to what, if anything, can and should be done. 99

—Nathan Glazer, sociologist.

M ost people believe that U.S. immigration policy needs to be reformed. In a March 2009 speech in California, U.S. president Barack Obama expressed his support for major immigration reform, saying "We have to have comprehensive immigration reform. . . . We do have to have control of our borders. . . . We have to combine that with cracking down on employers who are exploiting undocumented workers. . . . We have to make sure that there's a verification system to find out whether somebody is legally able to work here or not."[42] Three months later, in a White House meeting with congressional leaders, the president reiterated his support for reform, saying his administration is fully behind an immigration overhaul. However, while suggestions for reform are myriad, numerous immigration bills have failed to pass Congress in recent years.

Immigrant Numbers

Some people believe that current levels of immigration to the United States are harming the country in many ways and that immigration levels should be decreased. Mark Krikorian argues that mass immigration is not compatible with modern society. While it has been beneficial in the past, he says, mass immigration is harmful today because it reduces the rate of assimilation, undermines American sovereignty, threatens national security, costs millions of dollars of government spending on things like education and health care, and lowers the quality of life for Americans. He argues that the United States needs to decrease its levels of immigration. The Federation for American Immigration Reform agrees that current levels of immigration are harmful to the United States. It says, "Today's level of immigration is simply too high to be regulated effectively, too high to ensure proper interior enforcement, and too high to be consistent with U.S. national needs and priorities."[43]

In contrast to advocates of reduced immigration, others believe that the United States should maintain or even expand its current level of immigration. They argue that immigrants benefit the country in many ways. Jason L. Riley admits that current immigration levels do have some negative effects, but he believes, "when those costs are properly weighed against the gains, open immigration . . . still make[s] more sense than protectionism. . . . We still have much more to gain than lose from people who come here to seek a better life."[44] One common argument for continued high levels of immigration is that the U.S. population is aging and that this will slow economic growth in the future. Therefore, the argument goes, the United States needs to welcome more immigrants to replace retirees, in-

> **Some people believe that current levels of immigration to the United States . . . should be decreased.**

crease economic growth, and help the country provide health and pension benefits for its aging population.

Other advocates believe that the United States must accept large numbers of immigrants simply because it is impossible to keep them out. Explains Harvard University professor Nathan Glazer, "So limited are our successes in stemming this migration that we might do well to consider how we can guide it rather than staunch it."[45]

Local Versus Federal Action

Immigration laws are under the control of the federal government, however no major reform of immigration laws has occurred since 1996, and many people express frustration that the federal government is not doing enough to address immigration-related problems. Immigration organization NumbersUSA charges, "Congress and the administration . . . should be prepared to either rein in out-of-control immigration or be voted out of office."[46] With this lack of federal action, numerous laws have recently been passed at the state level to address immigration-related problems. According to a report by the National Conference of State Legislatures, the number of immigration-related state laws passed in 2007 was nearly triple that of 2006—240 laws compared with only 84 in 2006.

However, state immigration legislation is controversial. One critique is that local governments do not have enough resources to take on the job of immigration enforcement. In a 2008 speech Phoenix mayor Phil Gordon explained that because of a lack of federal action, local law enforcement is being forced to do more and more in regard to immigration enforcement, and that this is harmful to everyone involved. For example, he says, from 2006 to 2008, the Phoenix police department turned over more than 13,000 illegal immigrants to Immigration and Customs Enforcement. He maintained that among other things, such a situation costs local communities economically because of the money needed to arrest and jail illegal immigrants, and it impacts public safety because it diverts police resources.

> " [Some people] believe that the United States should maintain or even expand its current level of immigration. "

Another critique of local enforcement of immigration laws is that it damages community relationships. During a 2009 Congressional hearing, law professor David A. Harris stated: "Put simply, if state and local police become participants in immigration enforcement, people in immigrant communities will not trust them. Instead, they will begin to fear them, and to fear contact with them. They will fear that any encounter with the police . . . will result in investigation *of them*, and will focus on their immigration status."[47]

Treatment of Immigrant Detainees

The United States is widely criticized for the way it treats immigrants who are detained pending removal proceedings. Detention is the practice of holding immigrants suspected of unauthorized arrival, visa violations, or certain crimes or terrorist activities until a decision is made to allow them to stay in the United States or return them to their country of departure. According to Amnesty International, in 2008 the average number of immigrants in detention in the United States was 30,000. The way these people are treated is extensively criticized. Critics charge that detainees are denied access to lawyers and due process and receive inadequate care while in detention. In a March 2008 report, Jorge Bustamante, the United Nations special rapporteur on human rights of migrants, concludes, "[I have] . . . serious concerns about the situation of migrants in the country, especially in the context of specific aspects of deportation and detention policies. . . . The United States has failed to adhere to its international obligations to make the human rights of the 37.5 million migrants living in the country . . . a national priority."[48]

> **The United States is widely critiqued for the way it treats immigrants who are detained.**

ICE has agreed that the way immigrants are treated in detention has some problems and has stated its intention to correct these problems. In September 2008, the agency announced new standards that are to be implemented in all facilities housing ICE detainees by January 2010. In 2009 Cori Bassett, spokeswoman for ICE, reported that detainee treatment has been improved, with even greater improvement expected in the future. According to Bassett, "The care and treatment that some detainees receive does not yet meet our shared expectation of excellence, and we can all agree this is a reason for concern." However, she adds, "We have already made appreciable gains in improving the detention system by adopting detention standards and monitoring the compliance with those standards."[49]

Evaluation of U.S. Citizenship and Immigration Services

Much immigration-related controversy centers on U.S. immigration law and U.S. Citizenship and Immigration Services (USCIS), the government agency that oversees immigration to the United States. They have many critics. Detractors charge that U.S. immigration laws are outdated, impractical, and difficult for immigrants to understand and follow. Matt Welch, editor in chief of *Reason* magazine says, "There are few areas of American life where the laws are as byzantine, crazy-quilt, and Kafkaesque as those related to entering the United States from abroad."[50] Critics also maintain that USCIS is not doing a good job of processing immigrant applications and that, despite the fact that fees have increased, the backlog is significant and the processing times are long.

In a 2008 press release, USCIS defends itself, reporting that the agency has significantly improved its service and efficiency. It states that 50 percent more naturalization applications were completed in 2008 than in 2007, and naturalization processing time was reduced from 16 to 18 months to 9 to 10 months in that period.

Verifying Employment Eligibility

While it is illegal for an employer to hire an undocumented immigrant or other immigrant who is not eligible for employment in the United States, in reality many immigrants who are not eligible do work in the United States. Critics argue that a crucial element of immigration reform should be to prevent this from happening. E-Verify was created in 1997 as a free and voluntary way for employers to electronically verify the employment eligibility of employees, and has both supporters and critics. It is operated by the Department of Homeland Security (DHS) and the Social Security Administration (SSA). E-Verify is voluntary, however some states have passed laws making it mandatory for certain businesses. While DHS is encouraging expansion of the system, it has many critics. According to a January 2009 article in the *Wall Street Journal*, about 100,000 businesses participate in the program. Beginning May 21, 2009, federal contractors and subcontractors were required to start using E-Verify. DHS says it is "the best means available for determining employment eligibility of new hires and the validity of their Social Security numbers."[51]

> **Detractors charge that U.S. immigration laws are outdated, impractical, and difficult for immigrants to understand and follow.**

The American Civil Liberties Union (ACLU) contends that the system relies on databases filled with errors and warns, "Expanding E-Verify would require every employer in the United States to verify the eligibility of every current and prospective employee using a flawed system that is riddled with errors. This will guarantee that millions of Americans will be barred from working."[52] In the *Christian Science Monitor*, staff writer Alexandra Marks illustrates how errors in the E-Verify system can harm U.S. workers. She tells the story of Fernando Tinoco, who was fired from his new job at a meatpacking plant in Chicago only two hours after he was hired because the E-Verify system showed that he may not have been a citizen. Tinoco says that by the time he received a letter confirming his legal status it was too late to get his job back.

English Language Requirement

Many people argue that immigrants to the United States should be required to attain proficiency in English. Proponents of an English language requirement insist that English is necessary both for reasons of practicality—to get a job, conduct business, and communicate with others—and as part of assimilation. Michael Chertoff, former U.S. secretary of homeland security, discusses the relationship between speaking English and assimilation. He says,

> Knowledge of English is one of the most important components of assimilation. By learning English, immigrants are able to communicate and interact with their

fellow Americans. . . . Assimilation does not mean losing cultural identity or diversity. It means learning English and embracing the common civic values that bring us together as Americans and adopting a shared sense of those values.[53]

Others contend that immigrants do learn English and that it is unnecessary to make English a requirement for immigration. In addition, some argue that the United States should embrace its cultural differences, such as other languages, rather than trying to reduce them. Critics insist that cultural diversity, including language diversity, enriches rather than harms America. Says journalist Kathleen McDade, "Cultural backgrounds are part of who we are. Why should we not promote and celebrate them? . . . As long as people are willing to respect the laws of the land, I don't see a problem with this."[54]

Public Opinion on Immigration Reform

Surveys of public opinion consistently show that the majority of the American population believes immigration reform is necessary. For example, according to a June 2007 report by the Pew Research Center, only 7 percent of those surveyed believe immigration laws do not need changing. In a 2009 *Washington Post*–ABC News poll, 21 percent of respondents say immigration should be the highest priority issue for the federal government, and 48 percent say it should be a high priority.

Polls also show that a major concern among the American public is addressing the issue of undocumented immigration. The majority of respondents are in favor of addressing this issue by enforcing existing laws, increasing border security, and deporting illegal immigrants. Opinions on various forms of amnesty for undocumented immigrants are widely varied. For example, a 2008 Zogby poll found that only 21 percent of voters support creating a pathway to citizenship for illegal aliens. In comparison, according to a March 2007 *USA Today*/Gallup poll, 59 percent

> " The majority of the American population believes immigration reform is necessary. "

of those surveyed believe that illegal immigrants should be allowed to remain in the United States and become citizens if they meet certain requirements.

Lack of Agreement on Reform

The majority of Americans support immigration reform but there is no consensus on the specifics of what should be done. As a result, the federal government has been unable to pass any major immigration reform in recent years, and the debate continues over what should be done to reform U.S. immigration policy.

How Should U.S. Immigration Policy Be Reformed?

❝Mass immigration is undercutting our general prosperity. . . . Limiting immigration is common sense.❞

—Americans for Immigration Control, "Control Immigration for a Good and Just Society," March 6, 2009. www. immigrationcontrol.com.

Americans for Immigration Control is an organization that advocates reduced immigration to the United States and strict enforcement of current immigration laws.

❝On the whole, immigrants are an asset to America. . . . We benefit from the labor, they benefit from our jobs. Our laws should acknowledge this reality, not deny it. Let them in.❞

—Jason L. Riley, *Let Them In: The Case for Open Borders*. New York: Gotham, 2008.

Riley is a senior editorial page writer at the *Wall Street Journal* and author of *Let Them In: The Case for Open Borders*.

Bracketed quotes indicate conflicting positions.

* Editor's Note: While the definition of a primary source can be narrowly or broadly defined, for the purposes of Compact Research, a primary source consists of: 1) results of original research presented by an organization or researcher; 2) eyewitness accounts of events, personal experience, or work experience; 3) first-person editorials offering pundits' opinions; 4) government officials presenting political plans and/or policies; 5) representatives of organizations presenting testimony or policy.

Primary Source Quotes

66 The federal government has not done the job that it needs to do. . . . [The United States should] pass comprehensive immigration reform, and the federal government should be doing what it's supposed to be doing, which is controlling our borders, but also providing a rational immigration system, which we currently don't have. 99

—Barack Obama, Democratic Debate, Dartmouth College, New Hampshire, August 26, 2007.

Obama is the forty-fourth president of the United States.

66 Why not pass no immigration bill at all? . . . The system works in its way. The most motivated, tenacious, and enterprising immigrants . . . find a way around the barriers we erect. Once here, they help our economy . . . and subsidize our Social Security system. 99

—Jacob Weisberg, "First, Do No Harm: Why We Don't Need an Immigration Reform Bill," *Slate*, April 5, 2006. www.slate.com.

Weisberg is chairman and editor in chief of the Slate Group and author of *The Bush Tragedy*.

66 A final touch [to immigration reform] should be the declaration of English as America's national language. . . . All legal immigrants to America should know how to speak American! 99

—William Gheen, "How to Reverse Illegal Immigration in America," *Americans for Legal Immigration*, March 16, 2006. www.alipac.us.

Gheen is president of Americans for Legal Immigration.

66 Instead of passing laws that mandate English only . . . we should welcome the flavor that . . . [immigrants] will add to America. 99

—Monique Cunin, "English-Only Laws Negate Melting Pot Cultures That Have Formed America," *Daily Gamecock*, February 8, 2008. http://media.www.dailygamecock.com.

Cunin is a contributor to the *Daily Gamecock*, a publication of the University of South Carolina.

> ❝ E-Verify is free and voluntary and is the best means available for determining employment eligibility of new hires and the validity of their social security numbers. . . . Privacy is an integral part of . . . E-Verify. ❞

—U.S. Citizenship and Immigration Services, "E-Verify," March 11, 2009. www.uscis.gov.

U.S. Citizenship and Immigration Services is the government agency that oversees lawful immigration to the United States.

> ❝ Even if this system [of E-Verify] were workable and cost effective, we should not want it. 'Mission creep' all but guarantees that the federal government would . . . capture greater regulatory control over Americans' lives. ❞

—Jim Harper, "Electronic Employment Eligibility Verification: Franz Kafka's Solution to Illegal Immigration," *Policy Analysis*, Cato Institute, March 5, 2008.

Harper is director of information policy studies at the Cato Institute and author of *Identity Crisis: How Identification Is Overused and Misunderstood.*

How Should U.S. Immigration Policy Be Reformed?

- In a 2008 Gallup poll only **18 percent** of respondents believed that immigration to the United States should be increased, while **39 percent** believed it should be decreased.

- The U.S. Department of Homeland Security reports that in 2007, **660,477** people were naturalized in the United States.

- In 2007 U.S. Citizenship and Immigration Services sent **276,912** immigrants back to their home countries.

- According to the National Conference of State Legislatures, **206** laws and resolutions related to immigrants and immigration were enacted by state legislatures in 2008.

- The American Civil Liberties Union reports that nearly **300,000** men, women, and children are detained by U.S. Immigration and Customs Enforcement each year in one of more than **400** detention facilities around the country.

- In 2007 U.S. Immigration and Customs Enforcement reported that the average immigrant detention stay was **37** days.

- In June 2007 the application fee for American citizenship increased **80 percent**, to $675.

Decreasing Public Support for Increasing Immigration Levels

This chart summarizes changing views on immigration between September 2000 and July 2008, according to Gallup poll results. It shows that there was decreased support for increasing or maintaining immigration levels following the September 11, 2001, terrorist attacks, and since then support has gradually increased. Overall, however, a minority of people are in favor of increasing immigration to the United States.

Question: "Thinking now about immigrants—that is, people who come from other countries to live in the United States: in your view, should immigration be kept at its present level, increased or decreased?"

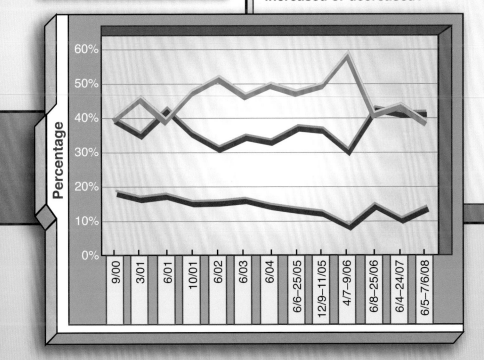

present   decrease   increase

Source: Polling Report, "Immigration," 2008. www.pollingreport.com.

- According to U.S. Citizenship and Immigration Services, the agency completed 1.17 million naturalization applications in 2008, **50 percent** more than in 2007.

Large Quantity of State Legislation Related to Immigration

This table summarizes the immigration-related state legislation that was introduced in 2007. It reveals high levels of state activity in relation to immigration laws, especially on the topics of employment, law enforcement, and IDs and licenses.

Immigrant-related legislation	Number of Bills Introduced	States	Enacted Laws	States
Education	131	34	22	17
Employment	244	45	29	20
Health	147	32	14	11
Human Trafficking	83	29	18	13
ID/Driver's Licenses/ Other Licenses	259	47	40	30
Law Enforcement	165	37	16	9
Legal Services	20	12	3	3
Miscellaneous	116	34	14	12
Omnibus/Comprehensive Measures	29	8	1	1
Public Benefits	153	40	33	19
Voting	53	23	0	0
Resolutions	162	37	50	18
Total	**1,562**	**50**	**240**	**46**

Source: National Conference of State Legislatures, "2007 Enacted State Legislation Related to Immigrants and Immigration," January 31, 2008. www.ncsl.org.

- In 2008 U.S. Citizenship and Immigration Services reported that **93 percent** of an employer's queries through the E-Verify system are instantly verified as work authorized.

Increase in Criminal Immigration Prosecutions

According to the following chart, the federal government has increased its efforts to prosecute immigrants who violate immigration laws. Federal prosecutions on immigration-related charges have increased since 2001, and were at an all-time high in March 2008.

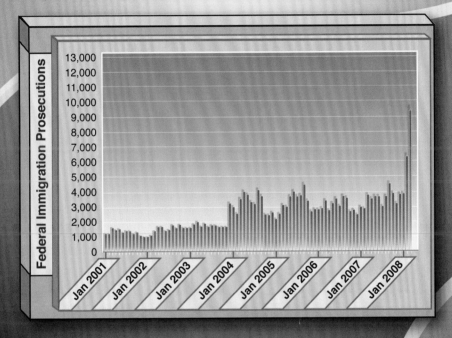

Source: TRAC Reports, "Surge in Immigration Prosecutions Continues," 2008. http://trac.syr.edu.

- As of January 8, 2009, **100,000** U.S. employers, or approximately **1 percent**, were enrolled in E-Verify.

How Should the United States Address the Issue of Illegal Immigration?

66Millions of illegal immigrants in our country belie the core principle of the rule of law and belittle the legal naturalization process.99

—Edwin Meese III and Matthew Spalding, The Heritage Foundation.

66Enactment of the kind of policies that would be required to fully eliminate the class of undocumented immigrants—whether through exclusion or through legalization—is politically unlikely and probably unachievable in the near term.99

—Linda Bosniak, Rutgers University professor of law.

With estimates of the undocumented immigrant population at approximately 12 million, most people agree that the United States needs to address this issue. Says Michael Chertoff, "Illegal immigration threatens our national security, challenges our sovereignty, and undermines the rule of law."[55] However, what to do about illegal immigration is fiercely debated. Areas of debate include: deportation, policing employers of undocumented immigrants, increasing border security, and providing a path to legalization. Also debated are the issues of free education for undocumented immigrants, guest worker programs, and the reasons causing these immigrants to come to the United States.

Deportation

While most people agree that attempting to deport all the undocumented immigrants currently in the United States would be unrealistic, some argue that the country should deport at least some of them. Not only would this reduce the current number of undocumented immigrants, but, as the American Legion explains, it might reduce the number in the future. The organization says, "The continuing threat of deportation and possible incarceration would serve as a deterrent to many who may be considering entering the U.S. illegally."[56]

Critics argue that deporting undocumented immigrants is not the best solution because it harms not only the immigrants and their families but also the communities in which they live. When undocumented immigrants are deported, families are often left without breadwinners and children without parents. In a 2008 report the *Legal Intelligencer* says that approximately 5 million children in the United States have at least one undocumented parent, so the potential number of children who would be impacted by deportation is large. Deportation can also harm the community when families are unable to pay rents and mortgages and need public benefits. Patricia Hatch and Katherine Fennelly of the League of Women Voters U.S. Immigration Study Committee argue that deportation is very disruptive to communities. They say, "Some communities where raids have taken place report abandoned housing, business closings due to lack of workers and dwindling customers, and dramatic drops in school attendance."[57]

Prevent Employment of Undocumented Immigrants

If work is the primary reason undocumented immigrants come to the United States, better enforcement of existing laws against hiring illegals would reduce illegal immigration, supporters of these measures say. They believe more diligent enforcement will deter undocumented immigrants from migrating and cause those already in the country to leave. A July 2008 report by Steven A. Camarota and Karen Jensenius of the Center for Immigration Studies shows support for this argument. The researchers find that following increased workplace enforcement, the undocumented immigrant population in the United States declined by more than 1 million in the year leading up to May 2008. The authors believe their data suggest that much of this decline is due to the increased enforcement. They conclude, "It is sometimes argued that illegal immigrants are so permanently attached to their lives in the United States that no amount of enforcement would ever make a large share of them return to their home countries. The findings of this report tend to contradict that view. . . . Enforcement seems to have played a significant role in reducing the illegal population."[58]

> Attempting to deport all the undocumented immigrants currently in the United States would be unrealistic.

Despite such arguments, some critics insist that strict enforcement of employment laws will not significantly reduce undocumented immigration. Catholic bishop Thomas Wenski insists that enforcement will not cause a mass exodus of illegal immigrants. He explains that "70 percent of the undocumented have lived in this country for five years or longer and have no home to return to. These people identify themselves as Americans more than anything else and would rather live here in the shadows than take their U.S.-citizen children back to a place they do not know."[59]

Border Security

One way the United States has attempted to reduce undocumented immigration is by increasing border security. Millions of dollars have been spent on the construction of a fence along the United States' southern border, and the number of border patrol agents has been increased significantly. In 2008 the U.S. Department of Defense spent $1.2 million on funding for the Southwest border fence. Overall, according to the White House, in 2008 the U.S. government spent $12.3 billion for border security and immigration enforcement. Chertoff believes that efforts to improve border security have been successful. In April 2008 congressional testimony, he reported that statistics showed a decline in apprehension rates on the southern border, which suggests fewer undocumented immigrants are trying to enter the country.

However, the many critics of increased border security insist that no matter how many new border patrol agents are added or how many miles of fencing are constructed, undocumented immigrants will continue to find a way across the border. In a 2008 report for Congress, researchers Blas Nuñez-Neto and Yule Kim state, "There is strong indication that the fencing, combined with added enforcement, has re-routed illegal immigrants to other less fortified areas of the border."[60] In his book *Dying to Live* author Joseph Nevins maintains that large increases in border security have not significantly impacted unauthorized migration to the United States. He says that while it is more difficult for unauthorized migrants to cross the southern U.S. border, 92 to 97 percent of Mexican migrants keep trying until they are successful. Critics also point out that as it becomes more difficult to cross the border, those who are successful are more likely to stay in the United States so that they will not have to attempt the crossing again.

Legalizing Undocumented Immigrants

Because of the large number of undocumented immigrants in the United States, many people insist that deporting them would be impossible and extremely disruptive to society. Instead, it is argued that the best solution is to provide a path to legalization for those already here. Angela Kelley, deputy director of the National Immigration Forum, argues that legalization would be beneficial because it would allow the United States to keep track of who is living in the country. She says, "We have 12 million people here living in the shadows. And . . . it is simply not tenable to not know who's in this country. We need a solution, where people will come forward, where they will register, where we will have a chance to screen them. . . . It's the only solution that makes sense, because, clearly they're not going to leave

> **When undocumented immigrants are deported, families are often left without breadwinners and children without parents.**

the U.S."[61] Advocates of a legalization policy argue that public safety would improve if immigrants were no longer afraid to report crime for fear of being deported themselves, public health would improve if they could seek preventative care rather than delaying treatment until they are sick, and the Department of Homeland Security could focus its resources on pursuing dangerous criminal aliens rather than undocumented immigrants.

> " If work is the primary reason undocumented immigrants come to the United States, better enforcement of existing laws against hiring illegals would reduce illegal immigration. "

However, many people are adamantly opposed to any type of legalization for undocumented immigrants. Some argue that this would be unfair to other prospective immigrants. Edwin Meese III and Matthew Spalding of the Heritage Foundation insist, "Failure to enforce immigration laws is deeply unfair to the millions who obey the law and abide by the administrative requirements to enter the country legally."[62] Another argument is that legalizing current undocumented immigrants will simply lead to more undocumented immigration. This happened following the 1986 Immigration Reform and Control Act, which gave amnesty to those illegal immigrants present as of 1982—approximately 3 million people. Following that amnesty, the number of undocumented immigrants in the United States has steadily increased to its current level of approximately 12 million.

Free Education for Undocumented Immigrants

States must provide elementary and secondary education to all, which includes undocumented immigrants. However, free public school education for undocumented immigrants is the cause of great controversy. Critics argue that because undocumented immigrants are in the country illegally, they should not have their education subsidized by taxpayers. In *Whatever It Takes*, Congressman J.D. Hayworth says that educating the children of illegal aliens costs almost $29 billion a year. He argues, "At a time when school budgets are under strain nationwide, it makes no sense to take on the burden of educating citizens of other countries to the detriment of our own students."[63] Others contend that children should not be deprived of an education because of their parents' actions. In addition, they argue that many illegal immigrants will stay in the United States regardless of whether they get an education, so it would be beneficial to the country if they were educated.

Guest Worker Programs

One often-suggested solution to the problem of undocumented immigration is to expand and improve guest worker programs. These programs allow immigrants to enter the country to work for a specific period of time, usually for an employer that sponsors them. The visa program for agricultural workers is one of the most well-known guest worker programs. Advocates of guest worker programs argue that the United States needs more immigrant labor than it currently admits, and this leads to undocumented immigrants filling jobs. They maintain that guest worker programs would allow these people to enter the country legally rather than illegally. Says former U.S. president George W. Bush, "We need to acknowledge that we will never fully secure our border until we create a lawful way for foreign workers to come here and support our economy."[64]

> **Millions of dollars have been spent on the construction of a fence along the United States' southern border, and the number of border patrol agents has been increased significantly.**

However, a primary critique of guest worker programs is that they are unrealistic. Demographer Michael S. Teitelbaum and Philip L. Martin, a member of the U.S. Commission on Agricultural Workers, maintain, "Decades of experience with . . . temporary worker programs . . . show that neither the programs nor the migrants turned out to be genuinely 'temporary.'"[65] Such critics argue that letting workers stay in the country permanently would be more realistic than allowing them to enter through a temporary guest worker program.

Address the Causes of Migration

Some critics argue that unless the United States addresses the problems in other countries that are causing undocumented immigration, it will be impossible to stop the flow of immigrants. Many people point out that some undocumented immigrants are trying to escape poverty, corruption, and human rights problems so severe that they will risk everything to come to the United States. Says Kevin Clarke, senior editor at *U.S. Catholic*, "The 'choice' they make to migrate is the choice between getting hit in the head with a hammer or a hatchet."[66]

> " Some undocumented immigrants are trying to escape . . . problems so severe that they will risk everything to come to the United States. "

Others argue that U.S. policy is to blame and that undocumented immigrants are coming in such large numbers because they are able to obtain welfare, free education and health care, and many other benefits. In the *New American* writer Charles Scaliger argues, "Even the long and bitter Mexican Civil War created no massive exodus of beleaguered Mexicans willing to enter the United States illegally, despite the fact that Mexico was far worse off than it is now, and crossing the Rio Grande unnoticed was far simpler."[67] He adds, "Something . . . has changed in recent decades. . . . That something is the burgeoning American welfare state. . . . A Mexican or other foreign national choosing to enter the United States illegally can expect to find a job, free medical care, free schooling for his children, and may eventually become the beneficiary of amnesty legislation."[68]

An Undesirable Situation

Linda Bosniak, professor of law at Rutgers University says, "Although parties to the immigration debate are bitterly divided over policy, virtually everyone agrees that the presence of a large class of unauthorized immigrants in the United States is undesirable."[69] Lawmakers and others continue to offer various proposals to deal with the issue of undocmented immigration, and these proposals continue to generate significant public disagreement.

How Should the United States Address the Issue of Illegal Immigration?

66 **What we need to do is make it impossible for illegal aliens to find work legally. . . . If we simply enforce the laws that we have on the books already . . . people are eventually going to give up and go home on their own.** 99

—Jessica Vaughan, "Senate Opens Debate on Bipartisan Immigration Package," transcript of discussion aired May 21, 2007, *PBS Online NewsHour*. www.pbs.org.

Vaughan is a senior policy analyst at the Center for Immigration Studies.

66 **Passed to reduce the 'pull factor' of employment, federal employer sanctions have not deterred illegal immigration.** 99

—Huyen Pham, "The Privatization of Immigration Law Enforcement," April 3, 2007.

Pham is an associate professor of law at the Texas Wesleyan University School of Law.

* Editor's Note: While the definition of a primary source can be narrowly or broadly defined, for the purposes of Compact Research, a primary source consists of: 1) results of original research presented by an organization or researcher; 2) eyewitness accounts of events, personal experience, or work experience; 3) first-person editorials offering pundits' opinions; 4) government officials presenting political plans and/or policies; 5) representatives of organizations presenting testimony or policy.

Primary Source Quotes

❝We must . . . secure our borders.❞

—John McCain, remarks at the 2008 National Council of La Raza Convention, July 14, 2008. www.johnmccain.com.

McCain is a U.S. senator from Arizona.

....

❝Enforcement alone will not permanently solve this problem. As long as the opportunity for higher wages and a better life draws people across the border illegally or encourages them to remain in our country illegally, we will continue to face a challenge securing the border.❞

—Michael Chertoff, testimony before the Senate Committee on the Judiciary, Subcommittee on Oversight of the Department of Homeland Security, April 2, 2008. www.dhs.gov.

Chertoff was secretary of homeland security from 2005 to 2009.

....

❝The benefits of an orderly earned legalization policy to unauthorized immigrants are clear. . . . The likely benefits to native-born Americans are equally significant.❞

—Patricia Hatch and Katherine Fennelly, "Unauthorized Immigrants: Earned Legalization," *National Voter*, June 2008.

Hatch and Fennelly are members of the League of Women Voters of the United States Immigration Study Committee.

....

❝The worst thing you can do if you try to control the illegal immigration is reward 12 to 20 million illegal aliens with citizenship and permanent residency.❞

Brian Bilbray, "Senate Opens Debate on Bipartisan Immigration Package," transcript of discussion aired May 21, 2007, *PBS Online NewsHour*. www.pbs.org.

Bilbray is a member of the U.S. House of Representatives, representing California.

....

66 [One] element of a comprehensive immigration reform is a temporary worker program. You cannot fully secure the border until we take pressure off the border. And that requires a temporary worker program. . . . It will help not only reduce the number of people coming across the border, but it will do something about the inhumane treatment that these people are subjected to. 99

—George W. Bush, "More on Immigration," address to the Arizona Border Patrol, Yuma, Arizona, April 9, 2007.

Bush was the forty-third president of the United States.

66 [A guest worker program will lead to] the exploitation of workers. . . . In the end, all that guest workers will get are short careers of transient servitude in the United States. 99

—Richard D. Vogel, "Transient Servitude: The U.S. Guest Worker Program for Exploiting Mexican and Central American Workers," *Monthly Review*, January 2007. www.monthlyreview.org.

Vogel is a journalist and author of *Stolen Birthright: The U.S. Conquest and Exploitation of the Mexican People.*

How Should the United States Address the Issue of Illegal Immigration?

- The Department of Homeland Security estimates that in 2007 California had approximately **2.8 million** undocumented immigrants, the most of all the states, followed by Texas with **1.7 million**.

- The Center for Immigration Studies estimates that the undocumented immigrant population in the United States decreased **11 percent** between August 2007 and May 2008.

- The White House reports that in 2007 U.S. Customs and Border Protection and Immigration and Customs Enforcement returned or removed almost **1.2 million** illegal aliens from the United States.

- In 2007 U.S. Immigration and Customs Enforcement levied **$30 million** in fines against employers, approximately **100** executives or hiring managers were arrested, and **4,100** unauthorized workers were arrested.

- The *Washington Post* reports that at least half of the **1.6 million** farmworkers in America are undocumented immigrants.

- According to the White House, funding for border security and immigration enforcement increased by **159 percent** between 2001 and 2008—from $4.8 billion to $12.3 billion.

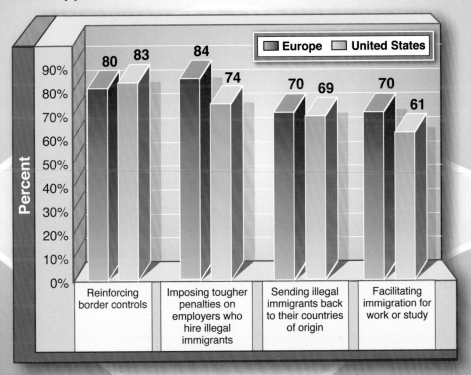

Significant Support for Measures to Reduce Illegal Immigration

This chart of European and U.S. attitudes on various measures to reduce illegal immigration shows that the majority of those surveyed support these measures. There was greatest support for reinforcing border controls and imposing tougher penalties on employers.

Support for measures to reduce illegal immigration

Legend: Europe | United States

Data (Percent):
- Reinforcing border controls: Europe 80, United States 83
- Imposing tougher penalties on employers who hire illegal immigrants: Europe 84, United States 74
- Sending illegal immigrants back to their countries of origin: Europe 70, United States 69
- Facilitating immigration for work or study: Europe 70, United States 61

Source: Transatlantic Trends, "Transatlantic Trends: Immigration: Key Findings 2008," 2008. www.transatlantictrends.org.

- The Immigration Policy Center reported in 2005 that 4 different studies of the apprehension and success rates of undocumented migrants crossing the United States' southern border suggest that between **92 and 98 percent** eventually get across the border.

Number of Border Patrol Agents Has Doubled

As part of its attempt to secure the border from undocumented immigrants and potential terrorists, the federal government has increased the number of border patrol agents. This graph from the Department of Homeland Security shows that the number of border patrol agents is estimated to have doubled between 2000 and 2008.

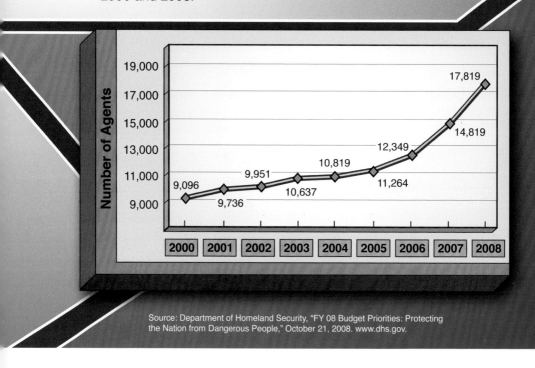

Source: Department of Homeland Security, "FY 08 Budget Priorities: Protecting the Nation from Dangerous People," October 21, 2008. www.dhs.gov.

- In a 2007 *Los Angeles Times*/Bloomberg poll of 1,245 registered voters, **60 percent** were in support of allowing illegal immigrants a path to citizenship.

- The *New York Times* reports that at peak harvest time, fewer than **2 percent** of immigrant farmworkers in the United States come through the country's farmworker program.

- The Pew Hispanic Center estimates that **73 percent** of the children of unauthorized immigrants in the United States are U.S. citizens.

Illegal Immigrant Population Is Decreasing

This chart shows estimates of the illegal immigrant population in the United States. It reveals that after increasing since 2000, the number of illegal immigrants declined between 2007 and 2008. Some people believe the decline was due to increased border security and efforts to prevent employment of undocumented immigrants. Others believe that the economic recession in the United States is partly to blame.

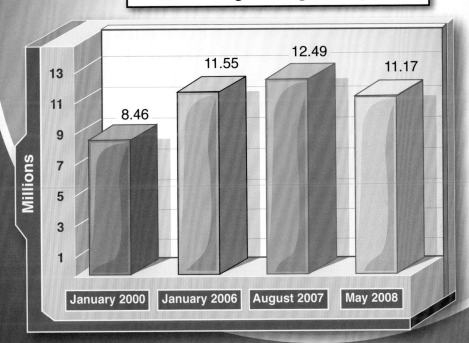

Estimated Illegal Immigrant Population

Source: Steven A. Camarota and Karen Jensenius, "Homeward Bound: Recent Immigration Enforcement and the Decline in the Illegal Alien Population," *Backgrounder*, July 2008. www.cis.org.

- According to the Department of Homeland Security, of the estimated **11.8 million undocumented immigrants** in the United States in 2007, **8.9 million** came from North American countries.

Illegals Deterred from Leaving by Increased Border Security

The United States has increased border security to prevent undocumented immigration, however it is argued that this may actually worsen the problem. Researchers have found that because increased security makes it more difficult for immigrants to visit home, they are more likely to make a permanent home in the United States. According to this chart, the probability that undocumented Oaxacan migrants will return from the United States to Mexico has decreased since the late 1980s.

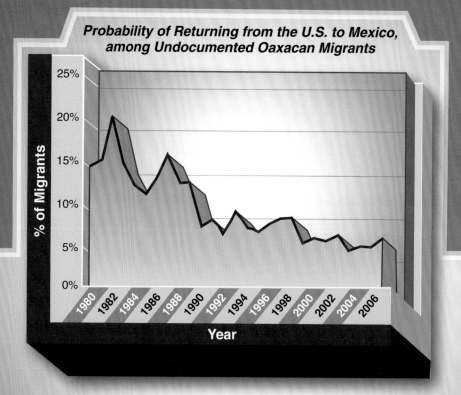

Probability of Returning from the U.S. to Mexico, among Undocumented Oaxacan Migrants

Source: Wayne A. Cornelius et al., "Controlling Unauthorized Immigration from Mexico: The Failure of 'Prevention Through Deterrence' and the Need for Comprehensive Reform," Immigration Policy Center, June 10, 2008. www.immigrationpolicy.org.

- In a 2007 USA Today/Gallup poll of 1,014 adults nationwide, **46 percent** of respondents said the United States should enforce its current immigration laws **more strictly,** rather than passing new ones.

- The Department of Homeland Security reports that between 2007 and 2008, the number of foreign nationals apprehended by the border patrol **decreased 17 percent**.

- A 2006 report by the Texas Window on State Government finds that undocumented immigrants contribute an estimated **$582.1 million** to Texas schools through school property taxes.

- The Center for American Progress estimates that trying to deport **10 million undocumented immigrants** would cost at least **$206 billion** over five years.

Key People and Advocacy Groups

George J. Borjas: Borjas is the Robert W. Scrivner Professor of Economics and Social Policy at the John F. Kennedy School of Government, Harvard University. His research on the economic impact of immigration is influential in immigration debates.

Steven A. Camarota: Camarota is director of research at the Center for Immigration Studies and author of *The Open Door: How Militant Islamic Terrorists Entered and Remained in the United States, 1993–2001.*

Center for Immigration Studies (CIS): CIS is a think tank that conducts research and policy analysis of the economic, social, demographic, fiscal, and other impacts of immigration on the United States. It supports an immigration policy that allows fewer immigrants but gives a warmer welcome to these immigrants.

Federation for American Immigration Reform (FAIR): FAIR is a national, nonprofit organization of concerned citizens that believes U.S. immigration policies must be reformed to serve the national interest. It works to improve border security and to lower immigration levels.

Immigration Policy Center (IPC): IPC is the research arm of the American Immigration Law Foundation. It works to provide policy makers, academics, the media, and the general public with access to accurate information about the effects of immigration on the U.S. economy and society.

Angela Kelley: Kelley is deputy director of the National Immigration Forum, an organization that promotes immigration.

Mark Krikorian: Krikorian is head of the Center for Immigration Studies and author of *The New Case Against Immigration*. He believes current levels of immigration are harmful to the United States.

Doris M. Meissner: Meissner is the former commissioner of the U.S. Immigration and Naturalization Service and a senior fellow at the Migration Policy Institute.

National Immigration Forum: The National Immigration Forum is an immigrant rights organization that advocates for public policies that welcome and support refugees and immigrants.

Jason L. Riley: Riley is a senior editorial page writer at the *Wall Street Journal* and author of *Let Them In: The Case for Open Borders*.

John Tanton: Tanton is founder of the Federation for American Immigration Reform and is an influential immigration activist who believes the United States should reduce immigration levels.

Chronology

1921

The Emergency Quota Act limits annual immigration from a country to 3 percent of existing U.S. population from that country. Eastern and southern European immigration is sharply reduced.

1942

The Bracero guest worker program allows Mexican workers to work on farms in the United States.

1996

The Illegal Immigration Reform and Immigrant Responsibility Act strengthens border enforcement and makes it more difficult for foreigners to gain asylum. The law establishes income requirements for sponsors of legal immigrants.

1986

The Immigration Reform and Control Act of 1986 gives amnesty to certain illegal immigrants who have been in the United States since 1982 and punishes employers who hire illegal immigrants.

1920　　1940　　1960　　1980　　2000

1924

The U.S. Border Patrol is created; the Johnson-Reed Act excludes immigrants from Asia.

1964

Congress ends the Bracero program.

1990

The Immigration Act of 1990 raises the annual immigration limit to 700,000 persons and increases the issue of visas by 40 percent.

1994

In California, voters pass Proposition 187, which prevents illegal immigrants from receiving most public services. The courts later declare much of it unconstitutional.

1965

Under the Immigration and Nationality Act of 1965, immigration quotas based on national origin are abolished and preference is given to relatives of U.S. citizens and permanent residents, scientists, and certain skilled workers.

2000
The case of Cuban refugee Elian Gonzalez brings public attention to the plight of illegal immigrants.

2005
Congress passes the REAL ID Act, requiring federally mandated standards of proof of identity for driver's licenses.

2003
The Immigration and Naturalization Service is abolished, and its duties are transferred to the new Department of Homeland Security.

2007
Congress fiercely debates the Comprehensive Immigration Reform Act, which includes providing legal status to illegal immigrants, creating a temporary worker program, and increasing border security. The bill fails to pass.

2000

2005

2010

2008
State and local governments pass an increasing number of immigration-related laws: Arizona makes employers responsible for checking the legal status of workers; Michigan stops issuing driver's licenses to illegal immigrants.

2004
The Intelligence Reform and Terrorism Prevention Act authorizes adding 10,000 new Border Patrol agents.

2001
After terrorist attacks on the World Trade Center and the Pentagon, focus increases on U.S. immigration laws and border security; the USA Patriot Act creates new immigration restrictions in an effort to fight terrorism.

2006
The Secure Fence Act authorizes the building of approximately 700 miles of fencing along the U.S.-Mexico border; millions of people participate in protests in response to proposed immigration reform.

Related Organizations

Americans for Legal Immigration (ALIPAC)

PO Box 30966

Raleigh, NC 27622

phone: (919) 787-6009

e-mail: williamg@alipac.us • Web site: www.alipac.us

ALIPAC is an organization that believes more should be done to reduce illegal immigration to the United States. It advocates enforcement of existing immigration laws and supports enforcement by state and local police.

Center for Immigration Studies

1522 K St. NW, Suite 820

Washington, DC 20005

phone: (202) 466-8185 • fax: (202) 466-8076

e-mail: center@cis.org • Web site: www.cis.org

The Center for Immigration Studies is a think tank that conducts research and policy analysis of the economic, social, demographic, fiscal, and other impacts of immigration on the United States. It supports an immigration policy that allows fewer immigrants but gives a warmer welcome to these immigrants.

Federation for American Immigration Reform (FAIR)

25 Massachusetts Ave. NW, Suite 330

Washington, DC 20001

phone: (202) 328-7004 • fax: (202) 387-3447

Web site: www.fairus.org

FAIR is a national, nonprofit organization of concerned citizens who believe U.S. immigration policies must be reformed to serve the national interest. It works to improve border security and lower immigration levels. Its Web site offers links to numerous publications and research studies.

Related Organizations

Immigration Policy Center

American Immigration Law Foundation

1331 G St. NW, Suite 200

Washington, DC 20005

phone: (202) 507-7500 • fax: (202) 742-5619

e-mail: info@immigrationpolicy.org

Web site: www.immigrationpolicy.org

The Immigration Policy Center is the research arm of the American Immigration Law Foundation. It was established in 2003 with the goal of providing policy makers, academics, the media, and the general public with access to accurate information about the effects of immigration on the U.S. economy and society. The center publishes reports on immigration, and its members testify before Congress on immigration matters.

Migration Policy Institute (MPI)

1400 16th St. NW, Suite 300

Washington, DC 20036

phone: (202) 266-1940 • fax: (202) 266-1900

e-mail: info@migrationpolicy.org • Web site: www.migrationpolicy.org

The Migration Policy Institute is a nonprofit think tank dedicated to analysis of the movement of people worldwide. It provides analysis, development, and evaluation of migration and refugee policies at the local, national, and international levels. The organization believes that national policy making benefits from international comparative research, and its Web site provides immigration research from around the world. MPI also offers the Migration Information Source, a Web site that provides immigration data from numerous global organizations and governments.

National Immigration Forum

50 F St. NW, Suite 300

Washington, DC 20001

phone: (202) 347-0040 • fax: (202) 347-0058

Web site: www.immigrationforum.org

The National Immigration Forum, established in 1982, is an immigrant rights organization dedicated to upholding America's tradition as a nation of immigrants. It advocates for public policies that welcome and support refugees and immigrants. The organization publishes numerous immigration studies and backgrounders on immigration and provides immigration-related information on its Web site.

Office of Immigration Statistics

Department of Homeland Security

800 K St. NW

10th Floor, Suite 1000

Washington, DC 20536

phone: (202) 786-9900 • fax: (202) 786-9910

e-mail: immigrationstatistics@dhs.gov • Web site: www.dhs.gov

The Office of Immigration Statistics develops, analyzes, and disseminates statistical information needed to inform policy and assess the effects of immigration in the United States. Its Web site contains statistical reports on various immigration topics.

For Further Research

Books

Edward Ashbee, Helene Balslev Clausen, and Carl Pedersen, eds., *The Politics, Economics, and Culture of Mexican-U.S. Migration.* New York: Palgrave Macmillan, 2007.

David Bacon, *Communities Without Borders: Images and Voices from the World of Migration.* Ithaca, NY: Cornell University Press, 2006.

Justin Akers Chacón and Mike Davis, *No One Is Illegal: Fighting Violence and State Repression on the U.S.-Mexico Border.* Chicago: Haymarket, 2006.

J.D. Hayworth, with Joseph J. Eule, *Whatever It Takes: Illegal Immigration, Border Security, and the War on Terror.* Washington, DC: Regnery, 2006.

Mark Krikorian, *The New Case Against Immigration: Both Legal and Illegal.* New York: Sentinel, 2008.

Joseph Nevins, photos by Mizue Aizeki, *Dying to Live.* San Francisco: Open Media/City Lights, 2008.

Margaret Sands Orchowski, *Immigration and the American Dream: Battling the Political Hype and Hysteria.* Lanham, MD: Rowman & Littlefield, 2008.

Jason L. Riley, *Let Them In: The Case for Open Borders.* New York: Gotham, 2008.

Rinku Sen, with Fekkak Mamdouh, *The Accidental American: Immigration and Citizenship in the Age of Globalization.* San Francisco: Berrett-Koehler, 2008.

Carol M. Swain, ed., *Debating Immigration.* New York: Cambridge University Press, 2007.

Periodicals

Judith Bernstein-Baker, "Effects of More Immigration Enforcement on Families," *Legal Intelligencer*, October 30, 2008.

Steven A. Camarota, "How Many Americans?" *Washington Post*, September 2, 2008.

Economist, "Keep the Borders Open; Global Migration," January 5, 2008.

Alan Greenblatt, "Immigration Debate," *CQ Researcher*, February 1, 2008.

Larry Greenley, "How to Fix Illegal Immigration," *New American*, March 3, 2008.

Jim Harper, "Electronic Employment Eligibility Verification: Franz Kafka's Solution to Illegal Immigration," *Policy Analysis*, Cato Institute, March 5, 2008.

Reed Karaim, "America's Border Fence: Will It Stem the Flow of Illegal Immigrants?" *CQ Researcher*, September 19, 2008.

Janice L. Kephart, "If It's Fixed, Don't Break It: Moving Forward with E-Verify," *Backgrounder*, Center for Immigration Studies, September 2008.

Alexandra Marks, "With E-Verify, Too Many Errors to Expand Its Use?" *Christian Science Monitor*, July 7, 2008.

Warren Mass, "Immigration as a Win-Win Affair," *New American*, March 3, 2008.

Edwin Meese III and Matthew Spalding, "Where We Stand: Essential Requirements for Immigration Reform," *Backgrounder*, no. 2034, Heritage Foundation, May 10, 2007.

Fred Reed, "Why Blame Mexico?" *American Conservative*, March 10, 2008.

Robert J. Sampson, "Rethinking Crime and Immigration," *Contexts*, Winter 2008.

Charles Scaliger, "Avoiding Extreme Solutions," *New American*, March 3, 2008.

Matt Welch, "Immigration Restrictions Hurt Legal Residents," *Reason*, October 2008.

Thomas Wenski, "Hitting a Wall on Immigration," *Washington Post*, October 20, 2008.

Internet Sources

American Civil Liberties Union, "Immigration Myths and Facts—January 2008," January 25, 2008. www.aclu.org/pdfs/immigrants/myths_facts_jan2008.pdf#page=1.

American Legion, "The American Legion Policy on Illegal Immigration: A Strategy to Address Illegal Immigration in the United States," 2008. www.legion.org/documents/legion/pdf/illegalimmigration.pdf.

Council of Economic Advisers, "Immigration's Economic Impact," Executive Office of the President, June 20, 2007. www.commerce.gov/s/groups/public/@doc/@os/@opa/documents/content/prod01_003086.pdf.

Jeffrey S. Passel and D'Vera Cohn, "U.S. Population Projections: 2005–2050," *Pew Research Center*, February 11, 2008. http://pewhispanic.org/files/reports/85.pdf.

Perryman Group, "An Essential Resource: An Analysis of the Economic Impact of Undocumented Workers on Business Activity in the US with Estimated Effects by State and Industry," April 2008. www.americansforimmigrationreform.com/files/Impact_of_the_Undocumented_Workforce.pdf.

Walter G. Rumbaut and Walter E. Ewing, "The Myth of Immigrant Criminality and the Paradox of Assimilation," *Immigration Policy Center*, Spring 2007. www.immigrationpolicy.org/images/File/special report/Imm%20Criminality%20(IPC).pdf.

Web Sites

Coalition for Comprehensive Immigration Reform (CCIR) (www.cirnow.org). CCIR is an organization that advocates comprehensive immigration reform from a human rights and labor perspective. It believes that reform must protect workers, reunite families, and provide a path to citizenship. Its Web site provides links to various fact sheets, publications, and research.

Immigration Counters (www.immigrationcounters.com). Immigration Counters provides numerous statistics related to illegal immigration in the United States. The organization supports legal immigration and is opposed to illegal immigration. It believes illegal immigration has a significant negative effect on society.

Truth In Immigration (http://truthinimmigration.org). Truth In Immigration's mission is to rebut legal and factual inaccuracies about immigrants and/or Latinos. It aims to serve as a watchdog for communications about immigrants and works to research and rebut inaccuracies about immigrants that are disseminated and promoted through the media, anti-immigration organizations, and political campaigns.

Source Notes

Overview

1. Robert E. Rector, "The Fiscal Cost of Low-Skill Immigrants to State and Local Taxpayers," congressional testimony, May 21, 2007. www.heritage.org.
2. *Economist*, "Keep the Borders Open; Global Migration," January 5, 2008, p. 9.
3. Federation for American Immigration Reform, "Questions and Answers About Immigration," September 2003. www.fairus.org.
4. Independent Task Force on Immigration and America's Future, "Immigration and America's Future: A New Chapter," Migration Policy Institute, September 2006. www.migrationpolicy.org.
5. David Friedman, "Immigration and Terrorism," *Ideas*, March 27, 2006. http://daviddfriedman.blogspot.com.
6. John McCain, "America's Immigration System Is Broken," *PoliticsOL.com*, May 13, 2005. www.politicsol.com.
7. U.S. Citizenship and Immigration Services, "USCIS Strategic Plan: 2008–2012." www.uscis.gov.
8. Bill Gates, testimony before the Committee on Science and Technology, U.S. House of Representatives, March 12, 2008. www.microsoft.com.
9. BigBadBart, comment on *USA Today* editorial "Our View on Immigration: Giving Visas to Skilled Workers Bolsters Economy," March 25, 2008. http://blogs.usatoday.com.
10. Amnesty International USA, "Refugees." www.amnestyusa.org.
11. Mauro De Lorenzo, "The Accountability Gap in Refugee Protection," American Enterprise Institute, May 23, 2007. www.aei.org.
12. Fred Reed, "Why Blame Mexico?" *American Conservative*, March 10, 2008, p. 35.
13. National Conference of State Legislatures, "The Executive Committee Task Force on Immigration and the States: Task Force Overview," January 8, 2007. www.ncsl.org.
14. Robert J. Sampson, "Rethinking Crime and Immigration," *Contexts*, Winter 2008, p. 2.

How Does Immigration Affect the Economy?

15. Steven A. Camarota, "Immigrants in the United States, 2007: A Profile of America's Foreign-Born Population," Center for Immigration Studies, November 2007. www.cis.org.
16. Raymond Keating, "Commentary: Before Reform, Know the Good Side of Immigration," *Long Island Business News*, May 23, 2008.
17. Quoted in University Communications, "Immigrants Add Nearly $1 Billion Annually to Arizona's Economy," *UA News*, July 30, 2007. www.uanews.org.
18. Edwin Meese III and Matthew Spalding, "Where We Stand: Essential Requirements for Immigration Reform," *Backgrounder*, no. 2034, Heritage Foundation, May 10, 2007, p. 7.
19. Jason L. Riley, *Let Them In: The Case for Open Borders*. New York: Gotham, 2008, p. 221.
20. Keating, "Commentary: Before Reform."
21. Media Matters Action Network, "Fear & Loathing in Prime Time: Immigra-

tion Myths and Cable News," May 21, 2008. www.mediamattersaction.org.

22. Thomas Sowell, "The Amnesty Fraud: Part II," *Townhall.com*, May 23, 2007. http://townhall.com.

23. Tiberio Chavez, "Always Looking for Something Better," in David Bacon, *Communities Without Borders: Images and Voices from the World of Migration.* Ithaca, NY: Cornell University Press, 2006, p. 117.

24. Rinku Sen, with Fekkak Mamdouh, *The Accidental American: Immigration and Citizenship in the Age of Globalization.* San Francisco: Berrett-Koehler, 2008, p. 9.

How Does Immigration Affect Society?

25. Jeffrey S. Passel and D'Vera Cohn, "U.S. Population Projections: 2005–2050," Pew Research Center, February 11, 2008, p. 12.

26. Lingxin Hao, *Color Lines, Country Lines: Race, Immigration, and Wealth Stratification in America.* New York: Russell Sage Foundation, 2007, p. 1.

27. Mark Krikorian, *The New Case Against Immigration: Both Legal and Illegal.* New York: Sentinel, 2008, p. 201.

28. Jack Martin, "Immigration and U.S. Population Growth," Federation for American Immigration Reform, July 2008, p. 3. www.fairus.org.

29. Riley, *Let Them In*, p. 39.

30. Immigration Policy Center, "From Anecdotes to Evidence: Setting the Record Straight on Immigrants and Crime," September 10, 2008. www.immigrationpolicy.org.

31. Jack Martin, "Illegal Aliens and Crime Incidence: Illegal Aliens Represent a Disproportionately High Share of the Prison Population," Federation for American Immigration Reform,

March 2007, p. 1. www.fairus.org.

32. J.D. Hayworth, with Joseph J. Eule, *Whatever It Takes: Illegal Immigration, Border Security, and the War on Terror.* Washington, DC: Regnery, 2006, p. 6.

33. Krikorian, *The New Case Against Immigration*, p. 110.

34. Sen and Mamdouh, *The Accidental American*, p. 66.

35. Federation for American Immigration Reform, "Immigration and School Overcrowding," October 2002. www.fairus.org.

36. Krikorian, *The New Case Against Immigration*, p. 173.

37. Justin Akers Chacón and Mike Davis, *No One Is Illegal: Fighting Violence and State Repression on the U.S.-Mexico Border.* Chicago: Haymarket, 2006, p. 167.

38. Hayworth, *Whatever It Takes*, p. 26.

39. Chacón and Davis, *No One Is Illegal*, p. 152.

40. Krikorian, *The New Case Against Immigration*, p. 13.

41. Charles F. Westoff, "Immigration and Future Population Change in America," in Carol M. Swain, ed., *Debating Immigration.* New York: Cambridge University Press, 2007, p. 165.

How Should U.S. Immigration Policy Be Reformed?

42. Barack Obama, speech at Costa Mesa Town Hall Meeting, Costa Mesa, California, March 18, 2009.

43. Federation for American Labor Reform, "Why America Needs an Immigration Time-Out," August 2003. www.fairus.org.

44. Riley, *Let Them In*, p. 224.

45. Nathan Glazer, "Concluding Observations," in Carol M. Swain, ed., *Debating Immigration.* New York: Cambridge University Press, 2007, p. 268.

46. NumbersUSA, "The Need for State and

Local Action." www.numbersusa.com.

47. David A. Harris, "Public Safety and Civil Rights Implications of State and Local Enforcement of Federal Immigration Laws," testimony before the House Subcommittee on Immigration, Citizenship, Refugees, Border Security, and International Law, April 2, 2009. http://judiciary.house.gov.

48. Jorge Bustamante, "Addendum: Mission to the United States of America," *Report of the Special Rapporteur on the Human Rights of Migrants*, United Nations Human Rights Council, March 5, 2008. www.unhrc.org.

49. Quoted in Tyche Hendricks, "New Report Blasts U.S. on Immigrant Detainees," *San Francisco Chronicle*, March 25, 2009. www.sfgate.com.

50. Matt Welch, "Immigration Restrictions Hurt Legal Residents," *Reason*, October 2008, p. 2.

51. U.S. Department of Homeland Security, "E-Verify," January 29, 2008. www.dhs.gov.

52. American Civil Liberties Union, "What's Wrong with E-Verify?" June 20, 2008. www.aclu.org.

53. Michael Chertoff, testimony before the Senate Committee on the Judiciary, Subcommittee on Oversight of the Department of Homeland Security, April 2, 2008. www.dhs.gov.

54. Kathleen McDade, "Should English Be the Official Language of America?" Associated Content, January 8, 2008. www.associatedcontent.com.

How Should the United States Address the Issue of Illegal Immigration?

55. Chertoff, testimony.

56. American Legion, "The American Legion Policy on Illegal Immigration: A Strategy to Address Illegal Immigration in the United States," 2008, p.

16. www.legion.org.

57. Patricia Hatch and Katherine Fennelly, "Unauthorized Immigrants: The Case for Earned Legalization," *National Voter*, June 2008, p. 11.

58. Steven A. Camarota and Karen Jensenius, "Homeward Bound: Recent Immigration Enforcement and the Decline in the Illegal Alien Population," *Backgrounder*, Center for Immigration Studies, July 2008, p. 9.

59. Thomas Wenski, "Hitting a Wall on Immigration," *Washington Post*, October 20, 2008, p. A15.

60. Blas Nuñez-Neto and Yule Kim, "Border Security: Barriers Along the U.S. International Border," *Congressional Research Service*, May 13, 2008, p. 32.

61. Angela Kelley, "Senate Opens Debate on Bipartisan Immigration Package," transcript of discussion aired May 21, 2007, *PBS Online NewsHour*. www.pbs.org.

62. Meese and Spalding, "Where We Stand," p. 4.

63. Hayworth, *Whatever It Takes*, p. 21.

64. George W. Bush, State of the Union Address, January 28, 2008. www.whitehouse.gov.

65. Michael S. Teitelbaum and Philip L. Martin, "No Such Thing as 'Temporary' Workers," *Christian Science Monitor*, December 12, 2005. www.csmonitor.com.

66. Kevin Clarke, "Let My People Stay," *U.S. Catholic*, September 2008, p. 46.

67. Charles Scaliger, "Avoiding Extreme Solutions," *New American*, March 3, 2008, p. 20.

68. Scaliger, "Avoiding Extreme Solutions," pp. 20–21.

69. Linda Bosniak, "The Undocumented Immigrant: Contending Policy Approaches," in Carol M. Swain, ed., *Debating Immigration*. New York: Cambridge University Press, 2007, p. 85.

List of Illustrations

Index

About the Author

Andrea C. Nakaya, a native of New Zealand, holds a BA in English and an MA in Communications from San Diego State University. She currently lives in Encinitas, California with her husband and their two children. In her free time she enjoys traveling, reading, gardening, and snowboarding.